Test to T

by

Ignatius Bukumunhe

ISBN: 978-1-291-81583-2

Every day in life we come across so many different people in various circumstances. One day you need a plumber or a motor mechanic or doctor, a solicitor or a banker, a teacher, a policeman or a politician. The list goes on and on. We also meet people we do not need, but are drawn together by common interest such as in sport, public houses, places of worship or the workplace. Some of these people you will trust. Some you will not trust. But how do you come to a decision not to trust or trust a certain individual? It's a difficult question and could be very tricky. The more you think about it the trickier it becomes.

Think about it for a moment. Close your eyes. Cast your mind many years past. You will probably remember something. Something nasty could have happened to you or a relative or a close friend of yours, involving a certain individual you trusted. This particular individual could have been a family friend, a close relative, your doctor, a politician, a teacher or a boss at work and older - much older than you. The incident may have gone away and no longer bothers you. On the other hand it may still linger on in your mind causing you sleepless nights, because it was so nasty. The memory of it is permanently etched on your mind. You just can't shake it off your mind. It keeps coming back every time you go to bed. You did not tell anyone about it at the time. You did not complain. In your mind you did not think anyone would believe your story. The particular individual involved was famous, well known and respected by the public. You were a minor unknown, unrecognised.

If the incident keeps coming back, robbing you of your sleep, and maybe even your appetite, there is one thing you could do to fight back.

As you lie in your bed, eyes closed, you will see this nasty individual. At this point turn the face of this nasty person into black and white and zoom it out down to your feet to the size of your most hated insect, if you like. Now say these words to this tiny face. **"YOU NASTY EVIL PEST, I DON'T FEAR YOU ANY MORE. YOU ARE NOTHING, NOTHING AND YOU CAN'T HARM ME ANY MORE."**

Repeat these words several times while stamping your feet on the face of this nasty person. Or at least pretend. Your fear will go away and will never come back. You can now start building self confidence and trusting some people.

Trusting those we should not trust could cost us the loss of a relationship, money or even lives. But people change all the time. The person you trusted Monday morning, becomes untrustworthy by Friday afternoon. You adore a man, put all your trust in him at 8.00 pm, and by midnight you find out that you made a grave mistake. The man you trusted is a wolf in sheep's clothing. Many a woman can testify and I am not being sexist here. Trust me.

As a baby you trust your mother 100%, and no one else. But as you grow you begin to extend trust to others. You choose your friends. You decide on which one to be serious with. And for the opposite sex you decide on one to be with for the rest of your life, because you have complete trust in each other. You get married.

This brings us to one interesting story. This is a story of one tribe in Africa in centuries gone by. In this particular tribe there was trust in the whole community to the level you could never imagine. They shared everything and I mean EVERYTHING. On a sad day they clapped together and sang sad songs. Come a happy day, they clapped together singing songs of happiness. If someone died, the entire village stopped everything, turned up at the funeral and contributed to all expenses in material and labour. While young men dug the grave, women were preparing food. The elders would prepare the body while the most senior would be discussing and deciding how the whole ceremony would be conducted. In a rare circumstance where an adult individual did not turn up to such a occasion, he would be noted. Missing more than three times the particular individual could be punished. A case in example is one man who showed no respect for the community. When Saul lost a son aged 19, nobody turned up to help. Saul and his wife had to do everything themselves; digging the grave and burying their son. In all his life, Saul had never bothered to attend any funerals, relative's, friend's or neighbour's, and remained a marked man.

This trusting in the community extended to parents and their sons and daughters, within a family. When a father deemed his son was ready for marriage he would go to the next village or beyond and look for suitable girl for his son. He did all the talking with the girl's parents, and all the leg work. It was only the two men who decided on marriage of the two young people. Sons and daughters had no part to play. The father would then tell his son to be ready for marriage. That meant the boy had to build his own house. He is not allowed to live with his wife in his, or, indeed her, parents' house. It is a well known respected taboo.

On the big day there would be feasting and music provided by a group usually from a different village. These are people who enjoy just providing entertainment to communities. In today's money, they would be the unpaid professionals. These 'professional entertainers' usually had a star dancer - a man on stilts. Children particularly found this very exhilarating and special and did not want him to stop.

One thing that you find very strange is that while all this was going on, there would be no sight of the groom or bride. The bride would be hidden away in the next village by her aunty, while the groom stays alone in his newly built house (hut). At sunset the boy's uncle would play a special tune on a drum with the palm of one hand and a stick in the other, alternately. Starting will be slow. slow, and then fast. He will then announce the arrival of the bride soon. The crowd will now look in the direction from which the bride is supposed to come with excitement, expecting to see the bride any moment. But the bride does not arrive until it is already dark - much later.

In darkness, covered by a veil, the bride accompanied by her aunty arrives. She will not sit down with the gathered guests. Her aunty will take her straight to the groom's house. No light is allowed in the house and it will stay dark all night until the next day. Bride and groom will talk to each other, feel each other and do whatever they want all in darkness. They will fall in love in darkness. Love can really be blind. They will not see each other till daylight next morning, inevitably revealing surprise to the two strangers having made love before seeing or knowing each other. It makes you think 'could I do that today'? This was done in complete **trust**. The two young people trusted their parents 100%. No questions asked, no complaints lodged, and they lived happily ever after.

Inevitably, as time went on, this system gradually died. This tribe found out that other tribes had a different system, involving dowry. This, they thought, was better as it enabled them to get something out of their daughter's marriage. And there was nothing to be ashamed of. Dowry came in the form of cows, goats, sheep and chickens to the parents. The other change was that the boy had to do all this by himself. He had to look for a girl of his choice. No more surprise for the boy or girl. The modern form of marriage had arrived. All they had to do is to make sure parents approved. This is a continuation of **Trust.**

In the City of Bradford, West Yorkshire, England, was a small very popular public house by the name of The Red Rum Inn. It was located in the West Bowling part of the city. Managed by David Herbert Smith and his wife, Anne, the Red Rum Inn was the talk of the town, attracting people far and wide. David Herbert Smith had changed his name from Nathan Herbert Smith as a result of his colleagues in the 5-a-side football team shouting NHS whenever he scored. He was the top scorer. At the time NHS was losing respect with the local community.

Kath Wilson was one of the fulltime barmaids in this popular Pub. Kath had a high IQ and would have qualified for a more responsible job. This 8 stone blonde young lady was the prettiest barmaid in town. She was said to have travelled to many parts of the globe, including Australia and Saudi Arabia. She had served on a cruise ship at one point in her life. Gail Storm was another barmaid. With brown hair and brown eyes, Gail had a baby face and would pass for Anne's 12 year old daughter. Yet she was already a mother to a 15 year old boy. Third was Tracy Green. She was a part time worker coming in at weekends and some evenings. Tracy was studying to be a pathologist. Another part time barmaid was Marilyn from Coventry. She was studying Sociology at Bradford College. This Marilyn Monroe look alike enjoyed being associated with her famous look alike namesake and one would say, she almost exploited it. She was an ever happy, cheerful and easy to talk to young lady. She did not turn up for every week-end as she was supposed to, choosing to visit her mother instead.

The Red Rum Inn was like a social club. The regulars trusted each other and were very happy together. And if a stranger walked in, they would all watch him or her very carefully. They trusted each other but would not trust complete strangers. One evening a stocky built man with a moustache and long flowing black hair at the back, but getting thin on top, walked in. He was a complete stranger. In a heavy Glasgow accent he started a conversation with one regular named Norman. Norman was American but preferred to be called African. His argument was that his great, great, great grandfather had been "stolen from Africa" and taken to America. Later, Norman changed the word "stolen from Africa" into "forced from Africa", in a slave trade act by the white man. Norman was always interested in some true heated arguments but would never hit anyone. The conversation between the two developed into a heated argument, and the man from Glasgow completely lost his temper. He went very close to Norman, and argued that it was a big mistake to blame the white man in general for the slave trade. He reasoned, and quite rightly, that not all white men were responsible for this dirty act. "Point taken" some one shouted. After a few exchanges of words the Glaswegian finally said Norman should blame the English. The Scottish are 100% innocent. The two men stood eye ball to eye ball weighing each other up. Moments later, and to everyone's disgust the man from Glasgow hit Norman on the chin so hard that he landed on his side but on the whole unhurt. This was followed by a big 'Woo' and "Are you OK Norman?" Norman did not retaliate. He got up, quickly finished his drink and walked out, saying he would never stoop to that standard of a man unable to understand reason, the lowest of the low. The regulars together asked this stranger who he was and why he did that. David, the landlord, was also involved and the stranger was eventually thrown out and banned for life. In the history of the Red Rum Pub, it was the first time ever to experience such a shameful incidence. This whole episode proved the regulars right not to trust complete strangers. Two weeks later word came through that the Glaswegian had been charged with GBH in a similar incident in another pub in the city. He received a 3 month jail sentence.

The following Sunday it was a different story but nonetheless very interesting. Something I remember so well. It was so strange. Sunday lunch time was not a time I would normally pay a visit to the Red Rum Inn. But on this particular day, a Nigerian friend of mine telephoned and suggested a lunch time meet at the Inn later. Half an hour in the pub two people walked in. One was a big fellow wearing a blue jean and a red jacket. I recognized him as fellow worker at St Johns Works at one time. Could not put a name to him but I knew that he worked in foundry section. The other wore all blue denum top and bottom, slim body and chains around his neck. They ordered drinks and stood by the counter. My friend and I were seated some distance away by the window. After a few drinks the slim fellow walked towards the toilet. Left was Ladies and right Gents toilet. To everybody's surprise he walked straight into the Ladies toilet. Coming out moments later all eyes were fixed on him. One man confronted him, taunting, and was followed by jeers from the rest of customers. He wanted to know whether this fellow could not read or see the clear "Ladies" sign. To which the slim fellow became very angry. Taking off the jean top and revealing a braless chest and small breasts, shouting, "What do you call these? Muscles or what?" For about a whole minute the man kept a steady fixed look at the bare chest having realized that the person was actually a woman, saying nothing. The man was very short and had to tilt his neck at about forty five degrees upwards to look at the woman's breasts properly. In the meantime several men wanting to share the instant free show, moved nearer to the woman. 90% of the customers were men. We (my friend and I) soon lost the sight as we were some distance away. From where we sat, we got only a moment's glimpse but the whole picture was later relayed to us by a bystander. You could hear a sudden rise of loud noise, the kind of which I've heard only from excited fans at a football match following a goal score by a home team. When the sound died the little man said to the woman "Thank you for a free show. In my young days, I would pay any thing to see strip tease. But I would not be persuaded to pay a penny to look at yours."

This made the woman so angry that she picked up a pint of

bitter and emptied it on the man's head. To make matters worse, the pint belonged to someone else not involved in the argument. She had picked the wrong drink. Confusion and anger followed. Some one took the initiative to cover the woman's chest and restore some dignity. Inevitably a melee followed. David the land lord struggled to keep peace. The big man who came with the woman stepped in. He grabbed the woman's hand pulling her outside. But before the pair left a man shouted "What about my pint?" The big man threw a five pound note and the two were gone. The two were not regulars and apart from me recognizing the foundry worker nobody else knew them.

There were quite a few notable regulars. Albert was probably the oldest regular and most critical of anything. Sometimes he acted in strange ways. Albert was tall, of medium build and looked very much like Tony Benn, the politician. He was also known for being a strong supporter of correct English Language. One thing that annoyed Albert was the so many interpreters employed just for those people who have chosen to live in England but make no effort to learn the national language. His suggestion was that a limited time, say six months, be allowed to learn the language. Anyone failing or refusing to learn the language, should be denied a job and dole money. On this point Albert had a few people on his side. But although many people trusted him, Albert had very little trust in anyone else. He would not trust any other driver and for that reason would not accept a lift in someone else's car. Albert regarded other drivers as fools and too careless to be trusted. If he himself was driving and came to a cross road, Albert would slow down and almost stop, even when he had the right of way, before proceeding. His observation was that so many drivers just drive ignoring every road sign, and completely disregard safety precautions. You can see some even signalling a left turn but turning right instead! This is madness. Albert always made sure that the other driver means exactly what he is indicating. Others don't even bother to indicate which way they are going until they reach the very point of turning one way or the other. According to Albert, when driving on public roads regard all other drivers as fools that cannot be trusted. Don't argue with them. Give in to whatever they demand. That way you will save yourself frustration and risk of being involved in an avoidable accident. The other thing Albert hated is driving on motorways. Speed is too high with so many careless drivers. Albert knew all the roads in the UK and could drive anywhere without using motorways or even maps. Here again is a question of trust

Then we had Ken, 70+, but looking much younger. Always smartly dressed up in black suit and a tie. A young woman was often seen in Ken's company. We should not forget big Frank. Frank was very popular for his singing. With his beautiful clear baritone voice Frank was King of Karaoke in the club. He sang a lot of old songs, from like the likes of Jim Reeves, Frank Sinatra, Nat King Cole, Elvis Presley and similar. Whenever he sang the "The Wonder of You" from Elvis he always ended with the the wonder of "**me**" instead of "**you**". If you know the song.

The most notable regular was a man by the name of Mr Tremble. He was addressed as Mr T most of the time. The very first time we met he introduced himself as a man from a place by the name of Wetwang. At first I thought it was somewhere in China. The name sounded Chinese or some place in that region. So I asked what turned out to be a silly question. I asked Mr T what part of China is Wetwang. Laughingly he asked me how long I've lived in Yorkshire and whether I have ever travelled to Bridlington on route A166. I had been to Bridlington from Bradford but never noticed the place or the route A166. Mr T went on to explain the small place in detail. As soon as I got home I checked it on a road map and there it was, the road A166 which Mr T had called route A166, joining A614 before reaching Bridlington. Actually I have never heard anybody else use the word "route" in the UK. What you will hear is road and not route. That was the beginning of our "friendship".

Mr T's choice of drink was Pimms, but often went for lager. This 7' 6" mountain of a man, with greying silver short hair never stopped talking. He spoke many times about trust, how he trusted everyone in the pub and how we all should trust him. He did so much talking without listening he was called a talking machine. He would ask you a question and would not listen to the answer. He will continue talking through your answer only to ask you the same question a few minutes later with exactly the same result.

Discovering that I originally came from Uganda, Mr T showed great interest. He wanted to learn more about Idi Amin and what exactly happened. He had heard a lot about Amin but never met anyone who was in the country at the time. When Amin expelled Asians from Uganda, he said, all TVs and Radio stations, all newspapers had, for weeks, nothing but Amin in this country. Pictures of arrivals at Heathrow airport of these Asians, some clutching little possessions having left all their wealth in Uganda, drew the British peoples' sympathy to them. It was Amin, Amin, Animal Amin, all over. But as I was in the country at the time, I must have seen the real picture of what happened there. He was interested in what was wrong with these people and what actually happened. Having heard Mr T say all that, I wondered whether it would make any sense me telling him what I knew with him being unable to listen. To my surprise, for the first time this talking machine Mr T did stop and LISTEN to what I had to say. The talking machine for a change switched off completely, listening to every word without interruption. Unbelievable, I thought to myself. Mr T was aware that being in the country at the time, we had the best chance of witnessing the event. My family and I lived only 100 metres from the Army Headquarters in Mengo two miles from the city centre of Kampala, the Ugandan capital. We could see soldiers drive up and down between the Army barracks and Army headquarters along the mile long Kabaka Anjagala connecting road, every day. We lived through Amin's regime. We saw him come. We saw him go; the same way he came.

In a military coupe d'etat Amin grabbed power from President Milton Obote, the first democratically elected Ugandan leader, after the country gained independence from Great Britain in 1962. Amin told Ugandans that Obote's government was so corrupt that it was not fit to be in power and promised to return to the army barracks after cleaning the country, and clearing Obote's mess, and continue as army Captain. He pointed out that it would take him 5 years to finish the job. No surprise to any of us, at the end of five years - just like so many African leaders before him, Amin declared himself Life President. He had a reason. He found a reason. He told the 20 million Ugandans that the best government for Africa is a military government adding that he was the best qualified choice/candidate, having had five years experience as a military ruler. Strangest among what Amin said on that day, live on radio and television, was *"Nobody can ever overthrow my government from power, and I know exactly the day I will die to the hour and the manner of my death."* One has to be mad or a complete fool to utter such words!

I met Amin on two occasions: first was at an agricultural show at Namarere near Kampala when working for a Farm Machinery Distribution Company. As he and his entourage walked past our stand, Amin showed great interest in our machinery. We were showing Agricultural machinery - tractors and implements. Second time was almost by accident. Me and a friend, and three friends - business associates - from Nairobi Kenya were having a drink at the Imperial Hotel in Kampala around 8pm when Amin walked past our table with two body guards. To our great surprise, as we stood in respect, he briefly stopped to shake our hands and saying that he wanted us to have good time before disappearing upstairs. This experience was more surprising to our Kenya visitors. To the youngest of the three, Henry, it looked like a dream. Henry could not believe that it was actually the real Amin shaking our hands. Excitedly Henry said it was real luck as he had never shaken hands of a President before. He went on to say that this could never happen in Kenya. President Kenyatta would never do such a thing. And if it was Jomo Kenyatta arriving, the hotel and surrounding area would be cleared of all humans.

Mr T was so interested in my story that he got closer and closer asking more questions. He wanted to know how I lived, about my job/employment etc in the country. I told him my story. My first job was as a salesman for Farm Machinery Distribution Company, selling Massey Fergusson tractors and their implements. After five years I resigned and started my own business in Import/Export. Later in the week Mr T asked me if I would like the idea of working with him in a business partnership. He was going to put up the cash having recently inherited a quarter of a million pounds from his mother as the only child. At the time I was in a job I did not like. The partnership would be doing export/import in which I had a good experience while in Uganda.

We kept on talking business for some time, for about three months, whenever we met - usually Friday nights, at the Inn. Many time he would drop in at my house bringing us (me and my family) ribs, eggs and bacon from his "mixed farm". More on this later.

The other part of Mr T was his great interest in Africa in general and its sportsmen in particular. Whilst he hated African politicians, Mr T admired African sportsmen. Names like the marathon man, Abebe Bikila of Ethiopia, the 1964 Olympic champion; the Kenyan middle distance runner Kip Keino; and Akii Bua the Ugandan 1972 400 metre hurdles Munich Olympic winner, with a new world record, were mentioned. In addition he mentioned a wrestler from Gambia by the name of Massambula. Massambula was popular, famous in the wrestling days of the likes of Big Daddy, Giant Haystacks, Mick McManus, Jimmy Saville and Jackie Pallo, among others on ITV Saturday lunch time sport in the UK. He said he regularly went particularly to watch Massambula at Bradford's St George's Hall in the 60's and Ken Norton was the commentator on ITV Saturday lunchtime World of Sport.

Then Mr T turned his attention on middle distance on British World Beaters. According to him the "S" factor made British World Beaters in middle distance races for both men and women. Starting with women Mr T could only come out with two names both hurdlers. Those were Sally Gunnel, Olympic 400 metre hurdler and world record breaker. The other was Shirley Strong a 110 metre hurdler and British champion at one time. Unfortunately, Shirley Strong was not strong enough to be a world beater. For men, Sebastian Coe, Steven Cram and Steve Ovett were untouchable in their days and real world beaters. Whenever and wherever they competed it was either of them winning middle distance races. Many times they came first and second, breaking world records in the process. These three shared world records in both 800 and 1500 metres at one time.

Incidentally, I bumped into Massambula's daughter, in a Bradford Social Club while writing this book. She introduced herself as Massambula's daughter as my wife and I were dancing. I do not have the slightest idea why she did this. My guess is that someone might have told her of my African origin. That was the only time we met. She was a 20 something year old, dark haired, white young lady.

Mr T and I kept talking business. At first I was not sure whether I should put my full trust in Mr T and go into business with him. Doing this meant I had to resign from the job in hand risking everything. That would be a very big step and probably unwise. As time went on I gradually started to trust Mr T more but still not completely convinced of the risk of leaving my job for the business with him.

Finally Mr T came to my home with details of the proposal of how we were going to work together. First thing was to look for office premises in the City Centre. Second we had to find a large detached house for me and my family. The reason for this large house was to make sure that clients from Uganda and other parts of the world would be accommodated and entertained throughout the period of their visit free of charge. The idea was to make them feel as comfortable as possible while in this country and let them know we care a lot about their wellbeing. This was good for business as they would not be pinched by other business people. This could easily happen if they stayed in a hotel. You don't want to take chances. The other reason, they would save on hotel accommodation costs and on returning to their respective homes/countries, they would spread the word everywhere, our hospitality to our benefit for more business.

We found a large office in Petergate, next to British Home Stores, first floor, Mr T wanted cash price for outright purchase. The officer in charge mentioned the figure which Mr T wrote down. After being shown what seemed to me too large for a starting business, Mr T suggested it was just what we needed. His idea was to divide it into three rooms: my office, a small kitchen and secretary's office. We left the place promising to return in a couple of days with an offer. Two days later Mr T came back to me to tell me about the office premises. He said he had spoken to the top man in Leeds and renegotiated a better price for cash. His advice to me was that when buying any big item to go to the very top and offer cash to get the best deal. The juniors won't and can't give you the best deal, they don't have the power and secondly their main interest in selling is their commission.

On Friday of the same week we went hunting for a house for me and my family. None of the first two were good enough. The following week Mr T picked up me and my family - the four of us - and we drove to Wibsey about two miles from the city centre. We found a five bedroom detached house with a huge garden. This was excellent. We all liked it. The only thing we did not like were the yellow painted windows, but that was a minor matter easily fixed. I was still a bit unsure about Mr T even at that stage. But when the gentleman showing us round said he recognized Mr T and thought him trustworthy, that put my mind at rest. I was relieved at last to put trust in him.

Next Mr T was to organise two credit cards; one for domestic expenses which my wife should use, and another for business in my name. Both were to be American Express. Arrangements had already been agreed in Manchester, he told me. Although everything seemed to be going smoothly and in the right direction, I still felt a bit of doubt once more. There was a pause. Mr T did not show for about ten days. When he showed up I asked why he put so much trust in me, why he was willing to do all that for me. I asked him who really he was. For the first time Mr T showed anger. He said, "Look Ignatius I'm harmless, I would not hurt a fly. I am not a politician. I am not a trade unionist. I am not a Thatcherite or Knockist nor am I party to Arthur Scargill. You are not the first Ugandan I have met. I trust you because I trust Ugandans. I don't trust Nigerians or Caribbeans. And I will tell you why I trust Ugandans. Several years ago I met Christian. A man of your size. Christian was a brilliant surgeon I met in Cornwall." I asked him if it was Dr Christian Nsamba. He did not remember his surname. By strange coincidence I remembered my best friend at school in Uganda while studying for Cambridge School Certificate at Mwiri was a boy of the same name and my size, and that would be about more than half a century ago. The Christian Nsamba I knew was a brilliant student, always top of the class. I understand he came to UK to study medicine at Cambridge. The last time I saw Christian Nsamba was at Mwiri. I heard that he qualified as a doctor, and at one time he was a top consultant somewhere in a Yorkshire hospital. I remember one Ugandan nursing student telling me that at one time she worked/studied in the same hospital as Dr Nsamba. As one of the top consultants he seemed to know everything. For all difficult questions Dr Nsamba was the first person to contact. The memory of the boy Christian I knew about 50 years ago, made me think. Maybe Mr T is telling the truth. There was no way I could check the facts. I had not met Christian since school days. There was no internet then where one could Google anything and find out what and where it was. Eventually I decided Mr T was telling the truth and should therefore be trusted. From then on I put all my trust in Mr T. We worked and reworked all the details of business strategy.

The plan was while I ran the Export/Import business in Bradford Mr T was going to start farming in Kenya. Arrangements for delivery of two 165 Massey Fergusson tractors and relevant implements, were underway. He had a friend farming 100 miles from Nairobi who was going to help him during the early days. This friend had lived in Kenya all his adult life and was then a Kenyan citizen and had married two local wives.

One Sunday afternoon Mr T came to my house and asked if I could go with him for a ride in his car. We drove towards Leeds from Bradford on road A647. One mile before Leeds city centre he pointed to a large building on the left and asked if I knew what it was. I did not. He then said it was a building where you don't want to be. Adding, *"You go there at Her Majesty's pleasure."* It was a jail - Armley Jail.

We continued driving around for some time until we came to a place where we stopped facing kind of a hill. I could see a farm a half to three quarters of a mile in the distance. Mr T, pointing to the farm, said it was his farm from where he often got us the eggs, bacon and ribs. Driving on he said we should not go there now. If we did we could not leave until late in the night. On the farm, especially a mixed farm like his, there is always something to attend to. My family would be concerned if we stayed too late and that's another important point, he concluded. As a family man you do not want to go home late.

A week later Mr T came to my house not in his positive mood. He told me how tragedy had struck his farm. Two of his horses had fallen into a ditch and it took firemen four hours to bring them out. But the biggest praise went to his farm workers who came in on their day off to help. They put in an exceptional effort to rescue these animals. He said he had never seen such dedicated men at work. He was very impressed. I suggested that he gives these men something in turn to remember. There were so many things he could do. My choice, among many, was a trip to the seaside. Blackpool was then the most popular seaside resort to visit.   Mr T agreed.

On Friday night when we met at the Inn, Mr T was in a very happy mood.   He told me how happy he was to see the boys drive off to Blackpool in a white self-drive hired minibus.   I was also happy especially as it was my idea.   I assured Mr T that he would get even more from his workers.   That's what I called indirect investment.   You spend some money to please an employee.   When an employee is happy he/she puts in double effort.   This is one of the best ways to run a business.   On the other hand if the situation is reversed and you do the sort of thing which makes a worker unhappy, production from such a worker will be reduced to the lowest level.   The business will, as a result, suffer.

But on Monday evening when Mr T came to my house he had very sad news.   The boys had had a nasty accident on return journey from Blackpool.   All were in intensive care in a hospital between Preston and Blackpool.   The minibus was a write-off.   The foreman had the keys which Mr T needed to get to his office.   The keys cannot be found.   The minibus cannot be searched till the insurance people have done their job.   Mr T was in a state of utter shock, and I felt very sorry for him.   Sorry on two accounts.   First it was my suggestion to send the boys to Blackpool, the second was we were so near finalizing the deal.   So when Mr T said he needed some cash quickly I obliged.   He could not reach his cash and could not break into the house either because of insurance conditions.

A few days later, Mr T came back with even worse news. The foreman had died.   But in spite of this, he added, we must press on with the plans.   It would not make any difference.

He said he would be able to go through this tragedy. At that time I suggested that we do it through a solicitor. His reply was that he was just thinking the same the previous night, and suggested that we do just that right away. Adding I should there and then ring my solicitor and make an appointment for a meeting as soon as possible. This I did.

When I saw him a few days later two more men had died. He asked for more money and announced plan B. Plan B was while he was waiting for insurance clearance and the return of his accountant's return to release the funds, he was going to Heathrow where someone who owed him quite a lot of money would pay a long standing debt. Mr T had told me earlier that the account for the funds from his mother's will had been frozen pending return of his accountant then on holiday in Morocco. He was expected to be back soon. He borrowed a briefcase from me and said the next time I see the case it will be full of cash - full of cash he repeated. He was going on Tuesday to Heathrow returning on Thursday night. Friday was when we should meet my solicitor, T. Clough & Co, Market Street, Bradford. We would meet at the Bradford Interchange at 10.00 am. The meeting was for 10.30. On the morning of appointment, Friday, I waited for him at the station. The 10.05 train arrived, Mr T was not on it. I rang my solicitor to say Mr T had not arrived on the train he was supposed to be. Solicitor's advice was to give it another half an hour. Two trains arrived, still no Mr T. Speaking to my solicitor again, I was advised to go to his office straightaway. At his office the solicitor asked if this man had taken any money from me. Of course he had. The verdict was this was, most likely, a conman and I should report the matter to the police. At the CPS I made a statement of several A4 pages.

21

The police also asked if Mr T had taken any money off me. They wanted to know if it was cheque or cash. If cash this man could deny having taken any money from me said the police officer. He man could even decide to counter charge you for false accusation.

The police also told me what the solicitor had told me earlier that Mr T was a conman. And that unfortunately the chance of recovering my money was next to zero. These conmen know how to con people. Some take time to study the victim over a long time. Win his trust and have the gift of convincing storytelling. All the story I put in the statement, the police said, had been meticulously planned by Mr T. The police was convinced the I could be one of several victims who fell for this trap.

I went home a very disappointed man. I had a sleepless night and many more sleepless nights followed. I sat down thinking what a fool has Mr T made me look like. How could I not have seen it coming? There was a time when I had some doubts about Mr T. In fact more than once , only to change my mind and put trust back to him, fooling myself that I had made the right decision. As I kept thinking about a suitcase full of cash, imagining what would have been, suddenly my mind brought back bad memories of the past and not very different. I remembered a similar incident while in Uganda many years gone by.

Me and four others had formed a trading company named Uganda Swiss Company (USCO). Import/Export was the main business and I was the only full time director, as a marketing manager. The office was next to the Belgian

Embassy in Kampala, capital of Uganda. All of us directors were interested in learning French to help us with our business and the Belgium Embassy had promised to help us. Just as we were struggling to learn French, a complete stranger dropped in. He said he was a Frenchman and could not speak English. He wanted to learn English so that he could do export/import with Uganda and Ugandans. We thought this was a great opportunity, just what we were looking for. It was a window of opportunity. This reminded us a story of one man in the village who wanted to cut down a big tree but could not find an axe with which to do the job. But one night as he slept, a strong wind felled the tree. We imagined how big our business would grow if we got on well with this Frenchman. We imagined being fluent French speakers within a short time. We imagined one day being in Paris chatting confidently with Parisians, negotiating business deals. We drew a list of what we wanted to achieve. Paris to us was the centre of Europe and so very useful. Among us we decided to do whatever it took to win the trust of this Frenchman for mutual interest. It was to us a God sent opportunity never to be missed. We went as far as suggesting that maybe we could put him up in one of our homes to save him hotel bills and continue learning French. This did not happen. The Frenchman stayed at the Kampala International Hotel.

In the meantime communication with the Frenchman was proving a little problematic. The only way we could communicate was by using a French/English dictionary. The Frenchman also had one.

On the third day the Frenchman invited us to his hotel - the Kampala International, now the Hilton Hotel. Five of us sat in his room and used room service ordering several rounds of drinks. The two parties agreed that it was better to talk business in a private room instead of sitting in the bar with all the other guests and customers. The Frenchman was even more enthusiastic on this I think than any of us.

After a few rounds the Frenchman told us he had a small problem. He wanted to change his US currency but was advised to wait a few days with a chance the value - the rate of exchange - might increase. He asked if we would advance him some Ugandan currency. Opening a suitcase full of US Dollars, in $100 denominations the Frenchman convinced us that he was talking serious business. Just by looking at the cash you could quickly imagine anything in the region of a quarter to half a million USD. Very impressed, one of our directors, the one with the shop, straight away said he would bring some cash the following day. He asked him how much he would like. The Frenchman only said quite a bit. He went on to say all that money in the briefcase would remain in Uganda to help "our business". That's why he wanted to change all of it and at the best rate of exchange he could get.

The following morning the Frenchman got the cash he wanted and suggested it would take about two days to change the dollars into Uganda shillings. On the third day he told us that he had not yet done the exchange, having been advised to wait two more days. We met every evening for a drink, at least two of us USCO directors. He seemed happy and relaxed. We were happy too, looking forward to the big business with France through this Frenchman. Among us directors we discussed a lot what we would order through the Frenchman on his return to France. We made a long list of the most urgent items. We made two lists: one priority and one a must have. The Frenchman would take our orders and since we trusted each other we should be able to do a smooth business for as long as was possible.

The next meeting was to be Friday morning in our office. The Frenchman was due to arrive at 10.30 am. All of us directors of USCO were there. When the Frenchman failed to turn up by 11.00 am we thought one of us would go and find him. The hotel was less than 50 yards from our office. The Frenchman was not in his room. We thought he might be waiting for cash in a bank. After a short wait, we decided to try later, after work, after 5.00 pm.

Talking to the Manager later that evening, we were shocked to hear that the Frenchman had vacated his room and had not even paid for the hotel bills. What made it worse was that the Manager was looking for anyone who might know his whereabouts, someone who knew him. Adding that he could not communicate in English but had been told that one evening a group of men had stayed in his room for quite a long time with a large bill for room service. A lot of alcohol had been consumed. That of course was us, unless there were others as well, which we doubted. But then you never know. The Manager asked how much and for how long we had known the Frenchman and if we trusted him. The Manager asked our help to look for this man just in case he had come to some sort of harm. To him we were first suspect. We avoided mentioning the stash of cash the Frenchman had on him.

We were very concerned about police getting involved. They would want to know of anyone who had something to say about the Frenchman. Realising they would have to start investigating by asking the hotel manager it became clear that there was no way we could escape being involved at some point. The manager would inevitably mention us. With so much cash on him the possibility of being robbed and even murdered could not be ruled out. Very worryingly for us; on finding the body we would be the first suspects. Our names - the Directors of USCO - would appear in all newspapers and the news media would have a field day. The press know how to spice up stories even before clear evidence is known. We imagined photos of all five of us, suspects in the murder of a French businessman/tourist. The more we discussed the issue the more we got worried. A bit of relief came when the first mention in the paper merely mentioned police were looking into the disappearance of a Frenchman who left the Kampala International Hotel without paying bills ten days ago as reported by the hotel. There was no mention of suspects.

The police wanted to talk to anyone who might have any information about the Frenchman, particularly anybody who had met or spoken to this man, as soon as possible. As we fitted this description we had no alternative but to report to CPS and give all the information we had. The officer at the station asked if the manager was aware that his customer had a stash of cash while staying at the hotel. We said we did not know if he knew. We did not tell him about the money. After a few more questions he said we were not helpful but he would call us back if necessary. It was more likely that we would go back to the police, he said.

Three days later we were called and asked to report to the same police officer as soon as possible. We had no idea what was going to happen. Although we were innocent of any wrong doing, being suspected of such a crime really bothered us. There was no mention of us being suspects, but we suspected we were suspects, the way things looked. In this case we could be detained in police custody while enquiries were ongoing. We just did not know what to expect.

At the police station we sat in front of the police officer to face the music. We were innocent, only worried because we had no idea what the police were thinking. We listened intently as the officer read a written report. The report had a lot of information provided by the hotel manager. There was a mention of a group of men who stayed at his room one evening consuming a large amount of alcohol. At the end of the written report the officer said that we were suspects. Repeating he went on to say that we had been suspects for some time. My heart sank. No body said anything, looking at each other.

Then there was a phone call, followed by a fax. As the police officer carried on the telephone conversation, I noticed that his face seemed to change from very sad to normal. He did not say much on the phone except, "Oh is that so! Are you sure. OK, asante rafiki" meaning thanks friend in Swahili. The fax was a full page. He read it about three times. He then turned to us and repeated what he had said before, that we were suspects and went on to say - until now. Explaining, the officer said he had been in contact with his counterpart in the neighbouring country - Kenya - they usually share information whenever necessary. The Kenya police had in custody a man answering the same description. This man had told some Kenyan business men he wanted to change US dollars into

Kenya shillings. Exactly the same story we had been told. But because intelligence had information from Uganda, the police arrested him. One of the men posing as a business man was actually working for the police in disguise. We left the police station very happy and relieved but sad for our loss.

It was a very big story in both Uganda and Kenya - eventually our photos appeared in both the Uganda and Kenya papers as innocent but wrongly suspected victims. It emerged that the Frenchman was not actually a Frenchman. He was an African from one French speaking country. Second and most important the cash in the case was fake. He also had many different passports from different countries. We wondered if this man might have been some kind of a spy.

The experience with Mr T in Bradford, combined with sad memories of the 'Frenchman' in Kampala, Uganda, together made me very sick. History had sort of repeated its self. I became unsettled and decided to take a week off work.

I travelled to London to spend some days with Erifaz, an old friend and former classmate in Uganda. At one time, Erifaz, Christian Nsamba and I were classmates in Uganda. Erifaz was a retired ambassador. I told Erifaz my story in full. I could tell the way he looked at me while listening was rather strange as if to express doubt of the truth of the story. True he could not believe the story, but not for the reason in my mind. He did not believe the story because he had exactly the same experience about 18 months before. Strange as things go, the man I described to Erifaz must be the same man who conned me. He had exactly the same description and similar story. We looked at each other for a moment of disbelief. Then we burst into laughter. How could we be fooled in exactly the same way! Then a friend of Erifaz dropped in. When Erifaz recounted the story to him, he said according to statistics it could not really happen, well a chance in 10 million, maybe, he reasoned. He first thought it was either a joke or a story we made up. Continuing, he said this is like the lottery. To which I replied "Well every Saturday millionaires are made through the lottery in the UK and many parts of the world. He asked me if I have ever won or knew anyone who had won a jackpot. Luckily I happened to know someone.

I knew one small man who never had a full time job. He lived on the dole and any extra cash he earned was for part-time work in a public house collecting glasses. One evening I was in a shop filling in my lottery card when he walked in. He borrowed £1 from me to play the lottery. The following Wednesday when we met in the same shop, he asked if he could borrow this time a fiver. I asked Tom why, what was he going to buy with £5. He said he wanted to bank £1,000,000. I thought the man was going mad. Then he went on to tell me that the £1 he borrowed from me netted him £999,995.00 - £5 short of a million. So with my fiver he could bank a million pounds. So there you are, I not only know one, I helped him towards winning the jackpot. Silence followed as even my friend seemed to doubt my account. But then Elifaz realised that I could not have made up this story. Several people become millionaires on the average, say, two or three people a week. Anyone could be in the lucky two or lucky three. You never know.

Returning from London my first port of call was the Red Rum Inn. It was a bit on the quiet side for a Friday, but most of the regulars were there. Still no sign of Mr T. David, the landlord, noticed I was rather quieter than normal. He asked me why I was quiet and where Mr T was. I told him the whole story of what had happened a week before I went to London. As he listened, he called over David Mahoney, who was a friend of Mr T to hear what I was saying. The two were surprised that Mr T and I had a secret - a secret business plan between us. I told them it was quite normal for people to be secret where important business is involved.

Then I got two surprises. First David Mahoney had his own story to tell, he told us that Mr T owed him some money, but much less than me. The second surprise came from Tracy, the barmaid. She said Mr T promised her a job at Leeds Teaching Hospital on finishing her course. She was studying to be a pathologist.

In the same week Mr T had disappeared Tracy had gone to Leeds Teaching Hospitals to enquire about the promised job . Mr T advised her to go and introduce herself to the hospital, talk to anyone - and just mention Mr T, and the job was hers. When Tracy got there nobody had heard of Mr T. She walked from the hospital in tears wondering how she could be so easily fooled.

So suddenly there we were, three of us victims of the con man Mr T in our popular place. I was the biggest looser. David lost less than £100. Tracy lost the expected job and hope. I lost nearly a grand. All the TRUST Mr T talked about all the time, had lost its meaning. All the TRUST we had amongst us, the regulars, was brought into question. The question was "How many more men we did not know in our midst were capable of doing what Mr T did? Mr T's name was all of a sudden changed to Mr C. C for conman. When the story got round, somebody swore to skin Mr T alive if he showed up at the Inn. Another suggested that Mr T should be hanged, drowned and shot.

There was anger everywhere. Alfred the oldest regular reminded us that he has never trusted anybody. He always maintained that belief.

Three months later I walked into the Inn one evening and there the landlord was, smiling as he saw me, saying he had news about Mr T. He asked if I wanted the good news or the bad news first. He said the good news was that Mr T had been traced. He is alive and well, and never felt better. The bad news Mr T was enjoying *Her Majesty's pleasure in Armley Jail*. He was done for car fraud for four years. The three of us decided to drink a toast to the news. This Armley Jail you may remember is where Mr T once said to me was a place you don't want to be. It was where you go on *Her Majesty's Pleasure*.

I later informed my friend Erifazi in London and he too was thrilled and relieved.

The regulars were very sympathetic with us especially me, having gone through all that with Mr T.

Old Albert was so incensed that he gave me a passionate lecture on trusting - test before trust. Reflecting on his earlier days, when he was a young man when there was trust in the majority of people, Albert noted that we now have conmen everywhere in all colours and guises. He did not trust anybody without proper examination. His strong words of wisdom were "TEST TO TRUST", in other words you do not trust anyone without first testing him/her. How you do it is entirely up to you. This is what motivated me to write this book. Unfortunately Albert is no longer with us. He has been gone for quite a long time now.

The effects of Mr T on the Red Rum Inn was very clear. Regulars dwindled down until the landlord lost interest in the business. David with his wife Anne moved out to a new pub six miles out of town in the area of Clayton. All the barmaids moved on and I was not sure where. But I knew that Marilyn moved back to Coventry after she finished her college course in Bradford. She wanted to be near her mum. The other two, Tracy and Haley could not be traced. Kath moved out of town, only, surprisingly to re-appear a few years later in a different guise. She got a job in the Chamber of Commerce as an executive officer. Perhaps we should not be surprised at Kath getting this job as we all noted her high IQ. Kath was both witty and pretty.

After I took redundancy from the job I did not enjoy, I planned to start my own printing business. I contacted the Chamber of Commerce for some directive/advice and was directed to an office in town. When I got there, the receptionist asked me to wait a few minutes for the Chief Executive Officer. Surprise, surprise there came Kath as pretty as she had ever been and still witty. Now I said to myself surely I can trust her without testing her first. Having known her a long time before, I saw no risk in trusting her. In any case there was nothing to risk. I worked with her in a new role very satisfactorily. Whenever there was anything -

information - that she thought might be of use she immediately passed it to me.

My initial decision was to do screen printing. A friend who was already doing it was prepared to guide me and help me in the early stages of the business. With a bit of luck, I was able to get suitable premises for rent near by. I paid the required deposit - three months rent in advance, and was very much looking forward to the day business would start.

Then I met an 'expert'. He was a man I had never seen before. He asked me if I had a hobby. I had a hobby in gold blocking which is slow and the machine could only be manually operated. This so called expert recommended that I continue with the hobby and make it into a full time business. He reckoned that screen printing had no chance of success. He added that I could continue working from home with gold blocking.

When I told him I had already put some deposit in renting a workshop he said it did not matter. The little loss of deposit would be compensated for by the profit I will make in gold blocking doing it full time. Back to my friend who was doing screen printing. He thought I was making a big mistake but then it was up to me. Do I trust this expert or my friend? It was a difficult decision but in the end I had to go with the expert. I think he was a civil servant.

My friend continued doing his business as usual. My Gold Blocking business went on steadily but it was not profitable enough. I continued learning new tricks to improve production and profit. In the meantime my friend was getting better and better. After three years my friend was doing so well that he was able to move to a much bigger premises four times the size. Within five years my friend was employing 20 people, winning award after award of excellence and young entrepreneur of the year, year after year. At the same time my gold blocking business was getting less and less profitable, to which point I regretted having decided to follow the advice of the civil servant so called 'expert'. I trusted the expert and not a friend with experience.

Then one day I met another print businessman. He was not actually a printer. He worked with several printers on a commission basis. He brings in an order to a printer and earns a percentage. We sort of loosely worked together for a period of about 15 months. He doing his and me doing mine. I found out that he was doing much better than me with much less work/effort. All he did was drive around and get orders. He was working from 11.30 am to 4.30 pm. while I started at 9.00 am until 5 or 6.00 pm.

But then business dried up affecting both of us. This friend came up with an idea I did not like.

He suggested that we change direction. He suggested that we could earn easy money with very little work if any. He went on to say that in one day, we could easily make £4,k. His idea was staging car crashes and claiming on the insurance. I said definitely NO. Insisting he said I should not worry. He knew how it could be done without me doing any thing. When I asked how, he said all I had to do was to sit in the car as a passenger and he would be the actual driver causing the accident. When the police came I would be the driver and he the witness. Still my answer was NO, NO, NO. I completely lost trust in him. I found out exactly what this man was - NEVER TO TRUST HIM again.

A few months after, this friend came to my house and called me from his car outside my home. He did not want to come into my house. He invited me into his new car for a ride. As soon as I sat in the car there was a very strong smell. I suspected drugs. He was now driving a spanking new car - a Mercedes 230 automatic. He gave me a ride, for about 10 minutes just to show off. He then asked me if I wanted to know how he was able to afford such a car - for cash. I said tell me. His answer was "If you want to be rich you should be prepared to take some risks. This is life man." he said.

I assured him that I was not prepared to take that kind of risk. We parted company and I have not seen him since. I understand he moved to another town.

The following week I happened to be driving in the Longside Lane area of Bradford 7, when I witnessed something spectacular. Three cars at high speed overtook me. About fifty yards ahead the second car overtook the first car and forced it to stop. It was like what I have seen many times on TV police chases.

On reaching the scene I stopped. I witnessed two big white males arresting two young people in the other car. The two young people were one male and one female. I asked the big man what was happening. He told me he was arresting this couple for drug trafficking. My memory went back to my print friend. It happened that the couple arrested had been grassed by someone as "a pay back". The arresting officer was in plain clothes but assured me that he was actually a policeman in plain clothes - him and a colleague. Even in crime trust is important. You can see. That very night I heard shooting. I did not think much about it. But the local paper reported a murder by shooting in the same area where shooting came from. The police had found drugs in the house. Drug based crime was suspected. A few days later, I met someone I knew who lived not far from the house. He told me he had visited the house and saw one man dead in a pool of blood and had called the police. This brought back very sad and frightening memories of the past while living in Kampala, Uganda, just after the fall of Idi Amin.

Bang, bang, bang. Three gun shots. I looked at my watch. It was two minutes past midnight. I felt a sudden cold tingle run down my spine. The shock kept me awake most of the night. The sound came so loud and so close that I thought it must be in our yard.

We had moved from the western part of the city to the eastern part to live with Uncle Henry. While on the whole Kampala was a not safe to live in, the eastern part was considered safer than the western. Uncle Henry's home was a large bungalow with two acres of land where he grew vegetables. Uncle Henry lived alone with a cousin, who did all the house work.

The following morning my niece, Jane, who was working in the next house as a house servant, knocked at the door with shocking news that Mr Shah had been shot dead. His 35 year old son was also dead. His wife had been shot too, but not killed.

I walked to Shah's house immediately. The time was 7am. The sight was so frightening that I came back straight away. In the living room was a group of about six African women wailing in a circle. Inside the circle was an Asian woman with a large wound in her leg in agony. Moving towards the bathroom I saw a young man, Shah's 35 year old son, lying dead on his back in a pool of blood. In the bedroom next door was Mr Shah himself, also lying on his back in a pool blood, dead.

Mr Shah was the Chief Accountant working for Uganda's Lint Marketing Board. The board's job is to organise the marketing of Uganda cotton to the world - a very important source of foreign currency for Uganda. As Mr Shah was the first Asian to be murdered, a friend suggested that it could have been a mistaken address/identity. Maybe the gunman was meant to visit our house. I got very worried. My uncle and I hatched a plan to enhance security. At the time although Amin had been overthrown two months before, gun shots could be heard every night followed by announcements of deaths the following day by the relatives of the victims. There were Tanzanian soldiers everywhere. They were friendly and kind to civilians, very different from Amin's soldiers. So Uncle Henry spoke to one Tanzanian senior soldier expressing our fear at night time. The soldier was very concerned. And it looked like nobody knew who was doing the shooting. Was it the Tanzanian soldiers, or was it the remnants of Amin's defeated army in hiding. The other theory was that a soldier could be hired to kill an old enemy as a pay back. In the end we got a Tanzanian armed soldier to stay in the house at night. We were sure we were safe at night from the night he started.

He was fed, showered every night and used our telephone to talk to his wife in Tanzania almost every night. We at least had trust in this soldier and felt much safer than we had ever been.

The big difference and concern was the new way people were being killed compared to Amin fashion/type. In Amin fashion an individual could disappear and the body would be found in the bush days later. In the new fashion, the gunman walks in to a house in the evening and shoots dead his target. The target could be a man with his family having a meal. The gunman had no hesitation in shooting the man at the table before walking away. If any member of the family showed any sign of concern or even begged for mercy, the gunman would turn on him/her. Dr Barlow, was a dentist, who was at one time my classmate. While he and family were having an evening meal, a gunman attacked them, and when his six year old daughter complained, she was shot in the leg before turning the gun on the doctor. Dr Barlow was shot point blank in the head in front of his family and died instantly. He was known to be outspoken, pointing out what he thought was not quite right to the authorities whenever he had a chance.

Me and family were so worried of the worsening situation that we looked for any opportunity to get out of Uganda at least for the time being. At the same time my wife's aging parents in England as well as her three sisters and a brother were all very worried about our lives. It was not easy to travel to England from Uganda at the time. We had to travel by road to Nairobi, Kenya to catch a plane to Heathrow London via Amsterdam. This was supposed to be a holiday and we hoped the situation in Uganda would have got better by the time we went back. Unfortunately that was not the case. Things got much worse and all our friends in Uganda were urging us to stay in England as long as possible, or at least delay our return to Uganda until the situation improved. It never did.

As our visas were only for three months we needed an extension if we had to stay longer in the UK. The situation in Uganda was getting more unsafe by the day. Murder by soldiers was far more prevalent than when we were in the country. The saddest news I received was just before Christmas 1979. In a letter I was told how my nephew had died from a single gun shot from a soldier in Kampala, the capital. He was travelling in a Peugeot 504 car with my two brothers and a friend. Fred was in the back seat between a friend, Moses, and his Uncle Israel. At 7.00 pm near the Norman Cinema on Kampala Road, soldiers stopped them and demanded that they surrender the keys of the car to them. It was not to be, and as the car pulled away, a soldier shot through the rear window. The bullet penetrated Fred's neck and stayed there. Seven hours later, at Mulago Hospital, Fred was dead. At the time the most popular car in Uganda was the Peugeot 504, apart from the Mercedes Benz. If I had been in Uganda the chances are that I might also have been a passenger in that car!

This tragedy was a big loss to our family and the nation. Fred was studying to be a doctor, in his first year at Makerere University. At Budo College he was not only a top sportsman in cricket, but he had a excellent academic record. Fred was also the Head Prefect in his final year at Budo. By now Fred would be one of the top consultants in the country. Whenever I remember this I get very angry.

Soldiers took so many lives of the same tax payers, who pay their wages, the very people the country needed most while they (the army) contributed NOTHING to Uganda's progress. With everything free - uniform, transport, living quarters, medical care and no tax to pay, they were a liability to the country. Besides, they were a law unto themselves. The police would not touch them whatever they did. The larger majority of Amin's army had been a bunch of men with little or no education at all and hated the educated. I remember one afternoon travelling in a minibus from Jinja to Kampala when we came to a road block. Armed soldiers stopped the bus and checked every one of us. They asked everybody so many silly questions and when someone said he was a doctor, he was ridiculed and humiliated. He was ordered out of the bus, served with a few punches before letting him back onto the bus. You could read the hate in their (soldiers) faces. Unbelievable. They were arrogant with no respect of human beings unless you were one of them. I was incensed, but of course I could do nothing. They always carried loaded guns and a law in themselves.

At the Home Office, the lady who interviewed me was very sympathetic. They (the Home Office) already knew all that was happening in Uganda. I was advised to apply for permanent stay in the UK. As my wife was born in the UK it made the situation simpler. This I did and all went well. We were allowed to stay in this country permanently. Before leaving the Home Office I was given some cash, which was helpful. At the time we were staying with my wife's parents in Lancashire, the four of us - my wife, me and two children, aged 9½ and 11 years of age.

We moved to Bradford, Yorkshire, in December 1979, where a friend of a friend lent us a small flat. We stayed there for about three months until we were offered a Council maisonette. This friend of ours, Peter, lived in Geneva, Switzerland and had a friend in Bradford. Having learnt of our plight, Peter suggested that we move to Bradford and work with his friend in business. This never materialised. But my wife and I got jobs and the children got good schools. Peter and I had met in Uganda , where he had come seeking to do import/export business. It was at the time when five of us were in the process of starting an export/import business. We got on very well with Peter. He was offered a directorship of our new company. Uganda Swiss Company Limited (USCO) was born.

USCO had one overseas office in Geneva which Peter looked after. The Ugandan head office was on Kimathi Street, Kampala, next to the Belgian Embassy/High Commission. Our working relationship with Peter was of the highest standard and we had complete trust amongst us.

Peter regularly came back to Kampala bringing with him some popular merchandise. We did very well from the very beginning selling whatever Peter brought. Most popular were office equipment, typewriters, calculators, watches and many more. In those days importing was not straight forward. There was shortage of almost anything you can think of and people did whatever they could to import goods. Suddenly the number of importers rocketed. The demand for ordinary essentials was very high. Ordinary commodities like soap, salt, sugar, bread, beer, cooking oil etc, were not available and ad to come from Kenya.

Daily, this new crop of importers having identified this yawning gap travelled to Kenya returning with the badly needed products. At the time manufacturing in the country was grinding to a halt, after the expulsion of Asians who controlled Ugandan economy. Travelling was by a 12 hour overnight coach journey (Akamba Bus Company) Kampala to Nairobi. An Import licence was not required for goods from Kenya. The country was starved of foreign currency. But the Uganda shilling was accepted in Kenya making it easy for importers of Kenya products. Other products outside East Africa needed an import licence. So before you could think of importing goods from outside East Africa, you had to apply for an Import Licence to the Ministry of Finance. Depending on who you were, or who you knew, there was no guarantee that you would get one. The big boys always got through easily. Top army officers had a real advantage. If your application for an import licence was successful, then you would also get an allocation of foreign currency for the goods, as per your pro forma invoice from the supplier. You then had to establish an Irrevocable Letter of Credit with a first class bank in the country of origin of the goods, in favour of the supplier. You had to pay the full amount on the invoice through your bank. The only alternative was to get credit from your overseas suppliers. But due to Uganda's reputation no overseas suppliers could give us credit. We found out the hard way after travelling to London at one time. The country was 100% mistrusted by the rest of the business world. Not even the so called friendly countries could help. At one time we thought that non western banks might be sympathetic and help Ugandan business in the form of bank loans, but we were wrong. While in London, me and a business partner approached one Middle East bank for help in our Import/Export business. We were only looking for short time bridging loan. We had the Uganda Shillings a plenty, but not Dollars ($) or Pounds (£). The manager politely advised us that we did not stand a chance simply because of the country - Uganda. No bank in the world was prepared to take that risk. That is Amin's regime for you.

When Peter brought merchandise, there was no need to apply for an Import Licence. This worked very well for us. Many people struggled to get import licences for months. It could take as long as six to nine months fighting with the Ministry of Finance. Priority was only for government first. The trouble was that the majority of business was engaged in import due to shortage of even the basic needs. Words like letter of credit and foreign currency were common knowledge. Even to people who did not speak the English language, the two had become part of the vernacular. The big surprise was when one of Amin's senior army officers went to the Bank of Uganda demanding to see this never-in-office, Mr Foreign Exchange. It surprised the whole nation when the story broke out that such a senior army officer had no idea what foreign currency was, when everyone else in the country knew. The country was being run by a bunch of uneducated and greedy people.

Another story relating to one of Amin's very senior officers is really laughable and pathetic. It is said that being unable to read or write he had been persuaded to learn at least to be able to sign his name on a cheque on opening the bank account. Initially he resisted. But after a gentle persuasion by a relative he reluctantly agreed. The alternative was a thumb print which he thought humiliating. He learnt just to write his name, and was very proud of this achievement. The only trouble was consistency. His signature varied and this lead to a real problem as proved later.   It shows how low were the rulers of Uganda then.   His CV read - previous job, tractor driver - operating a caterpillar D8 bulldozer.   Reading and writing were not a requisite, just like my Uncle Peter. Although he was illiterate he fought in Burma in World War II as a driver without any problems.

One day this very senior officer, sent a servant with a cheque after signing it, to collect cash.   It was quite a large amount.   But the signature did not seem to be genuine and was rejected by the cashier.   Returning without the cash the boy reported to the officer that the cheque had been rejected, adding that maybe there was not enough money in the account. This made the officer very angry.   He jumped up and down in anger.   He thought that it was humiliating, having been judged not to have money in his bank account which was not true. Next thing he did was to go in person to the bank.   With fury he demanded to see the Manager. Facing the manager across a desk, the army officer said to the bank manager, *"Don't you know who I am?   How dare you humiliate me the way you have done?   Don't you know that I am a senior arm officer?"* The Manager apologised profusely and tried to explain the situation, but the army officer would not buy it.   The Manager told the cashier to pay the cash, but he had to sign a new cheque there and then.   The Manager assured the army officer that that kind of thing will NEVER happen again.

A week later, the servant who had been in the thick of it took advantage of the situation.   He was the real winner.   He tore a leaf from the cheque book, forged the officer's signature and cashed a large amount of money and disappeared.   The bank had given up being consistent with the officer's signature.

I think it was Barclays Bank. The story does not tell us what followed.

But one can guess that the army officer, if he ever found out what actually happened, would be furious with the bank, and demand a refund. He would go in person and demand to see the Manager face to face once more. Maybe, being unable to read, he never found out.

The servant played a game of trust versus mistrust, squeezing in between. He knew exactly what was going to happen. He knew what he was doing. He remembered the words of the Bank Manager, "Such a thing will NEVER happen again." He knew the bank could never reject the cheque for cash from this particular army officer whatever signature appeared. He knew he would get the cash for sure. And he was right. The boy got the cash and ran away never to be seen again.

Many evil thinkers congratulated the boy on his action and thought he did the right thing. They thought the boy was smart. But I say it was theft, without doubt. It was also fraud.

Going back to old Albert's word of wisdom, we are all born with both *evil* and *good*. But the evil develops very slowly and will not show up till it is sure you are capable of understanding and believe in whatever it wants you to follow. As the two - the evil and the good - work together, between them decide which of them would take a certain individual. So much is at their disposal, they are spoiled for choice. According to Albert, all this is a balancing act. We have rain and shine, the poor and the rich, the beauty and the beast, light and darkness, the knowledgeable and the ignorant, water and fire, mountains and oceans - the list goes on and on. There are two side to everything and the two depend on each other. Take for example the rich and the poor. The rich need the poor to supply labour to work in his factory/estate. At the same time the poor needs the rich for employment. The poor would not survive without employment provided by the rich.

Without darkness light would have no meaning to us and vice versa. So whatever we do, the evil, like the good, is here to stay. And the good is even better when next to the bad. The poor and the rich will always live together, for poorer or for richer till the end of the world, some three billion years away. We will always need each other. There is no alternative. There are people in this world who will do everything to do nothing but expect to be paid as much as those who slave all day. And they are prepared to spend time fighting and disrupting dedicated workers. Many of these people do this all their lives. They hate a successful worker the very person who pays for their welfare money through taxation. Many have a particular hatred for the self employed. What a funny world we live in!

Final words from old Albert were that the devil seems to have a stronger hand than the good. It has an eagle eye to spot the weak from afar and can home in any time. Every house in the land is visited at least once without fail, by the devil. The devil could be visiting your home right now. The devil could have just left your home, or could be on his way to your home. There is no chance to escape and no home is safe.

The very last words of wisdom from Albert, however, were specially for me. He said to me he had not long to live, being terminally ill with cancer. I felt very sorry for him. Albert went on to say he liked me because I was a real gentleman and had respect for me. He then suggested that we meet midweek when the Inn was quiet, for a quiet talk.

The following Wednesday we met and had a table to ourselves. Not being sure what Albert had to say my anxiety grew as we sat down, having bought a drink each. A pint of bitter for Albert and for me one half of lager. Albert never bought a drink for any one, and avoided drinking in groups. This suited me. Albert was a 6 pint a night man. Mine was one and a half pints of lager, as has always been for the past 40 years, and still is today. Albert had a personal tankard with his name engraved on it, which only he used. The good thing with Albert, or shall I say credit to him, was that you could never find him drunk and he always walked away normally back to his home 100 yards away. He was always the first man to condemn drunkards and their appalling behaviour.

After a sip on his drink Albert leaned and whispered in my ear. There was no reason for whispering as it was quiet. But he was used to doing so when the pub was full of people and it was an automatic reaction. He said, "I want you to tell me all about your early days - childhood and your ancestors." To which I replied that I could go only as far as my maternal grandfather. My paternal grand father died when I was very small. I could have been as young as two. I have only a vague memory of him. I don't remember much at that age. Two other things still in my memory. I remember the twins born after me. All I remember is that they were dressed in off white similar long dresses with pictures of doves something Egyptian like. I also remember the youngest brother when he was born. He was born late in the evening and we had paraffin lamps lit. It was dark. Very dark. I remember voices of so many women most probably mum's sisters or neighbours or some relatives. A woman by the name of Kalende did the delivery work. Kalende was a midwife extraordinaire . She was not a trained in midwifery. Trained midwives would have been missionaries from Britain. And it was the same for doctors and nurses. Doctors, nurses, and midwives would have been working in the hospitals located in the capital or a big town miles away and certainly not for everybody. If you required hospital treatment you had to travel to Mulago or Mengo in Kampala the capital, some 85 miles away from where we lived. The twins had to be born in Mengo Hospital due to complications of mum's pregnancy. I am not sure how my parents were able to organise this, I only suspect that the missionary played a part in it. But also it is said that our father was a well organised, intelligent man just like mother was.

There were some special people with the magic touch to cure any ailments. Many acquired skills from the older generation in the family, keeping closed secrets all along. Special herbs were often used to effective results. Kalende was known to deliver babies in our area on a regular basis. Kalende was the most trusted female by a long way. She was the only one to do the job. On the night one thing that I particularly remember was the weight of my baby brother. I heard a woman's voice shouting "9 pound baby boy."

My father died when I was only nine or thereabouts, leaving **seven** of us children and our mother. The oldest , a boy, was about thirteen and the youngest a three month old-girl, with twins in the middle (a boy and a girl). Altogether we were four boys and three girls. The youngest, a girl, born soon after father's death, passed away aged just six months. Both parents were in their late thirties. Mother never remarried. Life was difficult for us. There was no social security. No single mother's allowances. It was all left to the widow to look after her children.

Having lost father's income, it meant extra work on the farm for all of us. There was some money said to come from insurance father had. It did not go very far and we needed some support if we were to continue with our education. Mother was determined that we all go to school and get a good education. Attending school was not compulsory. The government did not enforce it but to our mother it definitely was a must. Some support came from our grandfather and one uncle, Francis, in particular, helping in paying school fees for one of us children. Schooling was a costly affair as you had to pay not only school fees, but also needed new uniforms, notebooks, pens and pencils, etc every year. Travel to school and back was free - just 45 minutes walk each way. Getting up early around 6.00 am, you had an hour's work on the farm before walking to school Monday to Friday. Half Saturday was spent on farm work and washing our school uniform, dry them in the sun and finally pressing the same with a charcoal iron - there being no electricity. The break came on Sunday. Although we did not do any farm work on Sunday, church going was a must. School and church were then one and the same, though with different heads. Attending Sunday service was compulsory but we still enjoyed just being there, dressed in our best white Sunday uniforms singing church hymns we loved and without the pressure experienced in class room. On

Easter Sunday we enjoyed the specially learnt songs for the occasion. But anyone missing Sunday service would face punishment by a school prefect the following Monday. This would be any appropriate manual work. Usually cutting grass on the school campus. Sometime you would be ordered to pick a bucket full of coffee beans from the school coffee plantation nearby, during the coffee bean picking season.

Sounding all doom and gloom as it does, we actually had some very enjoyable times. Sports provided most of the enjoyment and pleasure. It could be football with a visiting school from some 20 miles, always on a Saturday afternoon. Dressed in school colours - black and yellow - the team was encouraged by the noisy cheering kids in a very special way, the moment they walked on the football ground, calling on their names one by one as loud as we could. This went on through-out the entire match following every action. If it was a corner kick, even before the referee awarded, it we all in unison shouted the word "corner". Incidentally the word corner is also used in our language, only spelled differently - koona. At the time we spoke very little English- just a few words. School education was conducted in our own language Luganda. Out of the six years in Primary School, only the last two, years 5 and 6, had some English lessons. There were no English born teachers whose mother tongue was English. And the English teachers had in turn been taught the language by teachers who did not have English as a mother tongue. Back to football. We seemed to know all the football rules now I remember, as we shouted in unison when we noticed any infringement. The "word" penalty was also often shouted, and when a goal was scored by our team the entire group would shout at the top of our voices the word "Goal" - spelt in our language "goolo".

Twice a year we had athletic competitions, which we very much enjoyed. Come to think of it when it came to long distance running I remember there was always one boy winning all the races. I think he was actually a small man. I was at the time about eight, but there were some boys in the school a lot bigger than me. One class would have 5-7 year olds mixed with as old as 14 year olds. School was not compulsory. It depended on whether or not parents were interested in the education of their children. Interested parents sent their kids to school as early as they could. At the time you had to be 5/6 to start school. There were no pre-school arrangements. Some parents only sent their kids to school when pressed by friends, sometimes it was already too late. It was not surprising to see a boy as old as 10 starting school and therefore mixing with the 5/6 year olds. So when it came to sport, the big boys of course performed better than the small ones. There is one particular boy I remember in Primary two (year two in today's money). He was not only much bigger than any of us, but also more developed mentally. He could read, do multiplications, additions and divisions. He was the only one in our class to do those things. For the rest of us it looked like magic. This boy was many years above the class. But the boy did not stay long with us. He moved out of the school and was never seen again.

In the school football team, I remember, the two big boys, Mutumwa and Bagimbe, were dominant. Operating as defenders the entire school had a lot of confidence in them. Mutumwa, in particular, was the only boy who could kick the ball from one end of the football pitch to the other and score a goal. He scored a few goals from that position. If the forwards were not scoring, this was the time for Mutumwa to shine. He almost scored every time the forwards failed to do so and we knew it. If there was no score by the last quarter of the match, we all shouted "Mutumwa! Where are you?'' We had confidence in him. And he delivered most of the time he was called upon to do so.

The school had a very strict discipline and the lightest offence led to heavy punishment. The headmaster was particularly a very strict disciplinarian. I remember one time when the whole school was punished. We had a trainee teacher who was so ugly that he became the talk of the town. Even children who never been to our school (and there many - schooling was not compulsory and parents were required to pay school fees which put some off) recognized him. One day during school assembly the head teacher told the whole school that an abusive letter addressed to a trainee teacher had been found in a classroom. It was anonymous. Suspecting one of the pupils, the headmaster demanded the writer to come forward there and then. He repeated the demand several times but nobody came forward. So he decided, without consulting the teaching staff to punish every pupil. He said, "The wages of sin will be paid". "Receive the wages of sin". Every time he decided on corporal punishment, the headmaster recited these words. So we all would know what was coming.

The punishment was eight strokes of the cane to every one. Children in the first and second year were exempt, so were the prefects. Eight prefects were picked to do the execution of the caning. To make matters worse we were ordered to collect from the bush the equivalent of canes. Each one had to bring

12 of these the day before the punishment.

This was not new. In extreme cases, where the crime committed was thought very severe, a teacher would administer strokes of the cane to the offender. One big boy was caught stealing clothing belonging to a teacher's wife. This was considered very serious. This boy was not only the best footballer/striker in the whole school, but also the football captain, and deputy head prefect. Before caning the boy, the teacher emptied a bucket of water on his bottom. Then as you might have guessed the head teacher recited the usual words "The wages of sin must be paid" The boy was also stripped of his captaincy.

In all schools discipline was **VERY IMPORTANT,** BOTH TO TEACHERS AND PARENTS. If a pupil misbehaved and was punished, he would have no sympathy from parents no matter how severe the punishment was. If you went crying complaining to your parents expecting sympathy and support, after punishment from your teacher, most likely you will get another one from your dad. So to save yourself double punishment, you kept your mouth shut no matter how much it hurt. Those were the days of our time. And it was not just our school. It was the same story was all over the country.

Months later we were told that the boy had done it again. This time he was expelled from school. The only good thing is that this time he did not "pay the wages of sin" corporal punishment. This was a big loss to us. The boy was very popular as a footballer. As a forward (striker in today's money) he scored many goals. He took all free kicks, corners and penalty kicks. He was the only one to score directly from a corner kick. To this day I still don't know how he did it. He must have bent it like Beckham!

Although as a small boy I cannot forget the head master's cruelty, the most memorable experience is the more cruel 'mother nature'. The most frightening experience was while I was returning home from school one evening. Walking home with about three quarters of a mile to go it started raining. The first thing I saw was a very bright rainbow. Then, it got darker and darker and the rainbow disappeared. The heavens opened with a fury. Strong wind, hail stones, thunder, heavy rain came down like I had never seen before. In those days if you found yourself in the rain, away from home, all you had to do was to seek refuge in the nearest house you found. The occupants may not know you or you may not know them. It didn't matter. As long as you were there because of rain you would be welcome to stay till it stopped raining.

So I entered the nearest house by the road. There were three men in the house, one of whom I recognised. He was a distant relative of my mother. The rain got heavier, the wind got stronger, and the thunder got louder. With the strong wind the roof of the house started moving up and down perilously. I asked the three men in the house what they were going to do about the roof. One of them suggested that they stand up and hold the roof firmly to stop it being ripped off the house by the strong wind. They all agreed and did just that. It looked like the wind would blow the roof off the house anytime. I was very frightened. It was a small house - a bungalow - with a corrugated iron roof. The most frightening moment was when the three men holding the roof, seemed to be lifted up by the force of the strong wind. The three men seemed to be lifted up and down fighting the elements as they hung on the roof. They fought very hard against the wind by holding the roof down with all their energy. It was up and down, up and down for quite a while. One moment even their feet are not touching the ground, then down to the ground. It looked like the men would lose the battle any time and they would be carried away with the roof as they held to it. This would mean the rest of the house being destroyed and our lives in real danger. Luckily, the wind suddenly subsided and the three men now were standing with their feet on the ground still holding the roof. But the thunder continued for some time.

When I left the house after the storm I saw three houses nearby had had their roofs ripped off. I am sure if the three men were not there to do what they did, the house in which I had taken refuge would have had the same fate. Trees and crops had been fallen and there was chaos everywhere. On my way home I noticed more houses damaged by falling trees. One house had been completely flattened. I don't think anyone in that house would have survived. With all this in my mind, walking towards home, I dreaded what I would find. I thought we might not have a home anymore. Luckily our house was still there intact. Our house had strong a structure with a solid foundation better than many houses around. Mother was there as usual waiting for my return from school; she could hardly believe my story. It was not until one of the men in the house I stayed during the storm- a distant relative - related the story some days after, that she was convinced I was actually telling the truth. The man had another story to tell us. His sister's house which was not far from where we had been, had a big tree fall on it destroying it. She was very lucky to be alive. By contrast during normal rain, as children we always ran out in it having fun . It was like having a shower. This we did so many times without trouble as the rain was gentle most of the time.

Trust or no trust, nature rules. We are all part of it and must follow its rules. As a matter of fact, we have no choice. Another year, I don't remember how old I was, locusts came. Trillions and trillions of them. So many that the sun was completely obliterated. I had gone to collect water from a well near our home. The well was surrounded by tall trees with scrubby brush around it. Inside the enclosure was a small space where you could see the sky but not the sides because of the bushes. Drawing water from the well the reflection of the sky and clouds could be seen in the water. As kids we used to enjoy looking at the sky through the water's reflection. On that day when I tried to look at the sky through the reflection it was all dark. I thought they were clouds. Then I heard some strange noises. Leaving the well and out of the bush I noticed a swarm of locusts in their trillions in the sky. No sun shone, I could not see the sky or the sun. Swarms of locust spread across the sky like thick cloud.

The locusts ate everything green. All the trees and bushes were left bare, only the Mivule trees (also known as Iroko or African Teak) were spared. These gigantic trees were special. They were the biggest, tallest, no insect/ants could touch them and they produced the best timber for furniture and building bridges. These trees were regarded too good for ordinary buildings for which cheaper alternatives were readily available. From our home extending may be 15 to 20 miles you could count 10 to 30 of these trees. Unfortunately this is no longer the case. It looks like as much as 90% of these magnificent trees are gone. So many saw mills were in the area for so long that the timber market where this particular tree was gold eventually became endangered, leading to its demise. Neither the Government nor the people took trouble to preserve and maintain the tree. The country could do with re-planting of these trees. They produced seeds every end of year when they shed their leaves. During the hottest months of the year, December and January, seeds in a cylinder/bag about 80x20 mm always fell down spreading over a wide area rotting after a few days. Since these trees were never planted (*Gyamera Gyene*), it was taken for granted that they would always spring back. The term *Gyamera Gyene* was used to explain how these trees came about to be there in the first place. It was in answer to the question by the first Briton in the area. The trees were predominant in Busoga. On hearing this, some people in Buganda did not like the answer. They would have preferred to tell the Briton that the trees were planted by us, and thus claim ownership. That would have been a lie. *"Gyamera Gyene" was an honest answer.* The main argument against *Gaymera Gyene* was that saw millers freely cut down hundreds of these trees making a real fortune and the locals got nothing out of it. Britons were in charge. The country, as a British Colony, was being governed from London. The saw millers were British and therefore Britain took the advantage. It was only when people started registering land ownership, that whatever was on it belonged to them, including these trees.

Locusts destroyed the rest of the crops, and in a space of just one week they were nowhere to be seen. Then suddenly, small baby locusts were seen walking/hopping everywhere. Locusts had laid eggs which hatched bringing a new generation of locusts.

The biggest effect of the invasion was food shortage eventually. The short term advantage was that locusts were a source of protein for all - animals, birds and people. The baby locusts were a delicacy. The adult locusts were hated for destroying crops but were also food with useful protein. They were eaten fried, peppered and salted. The baby locusts joined the food chain about a week later.

Locusts are an invading army. They come, cause havoc and disappear in days. The rest of the insect kingdom are always around. As a child this is the only occasion I remember locusts invading. I am sure this was not the only time the country saw these insects. There are other millions of insects of course. There are those that leave you with a nasty sting and no poison like some ants. Then you have bees and spiders. These cause a swollen part of your body but the pain and even poison can be tolerated for a short time. I've been bitten and seen people bitten by these two, as a child. I remember swelling from the sting of a bee and a spider. I have no memory of any medication being administered. Then there are ants that eat almost anything in the house and outside; wood, cloth, paper, even small plants. Then of course you have house flies, which are just a nuisance with no sting. You may be eating or drinking only to find a fly in your cup of tea, soup or food. Although looking at so many types, colours and sizes of insects was in itself satisfying, but it was birds that excited me most.

As early as 6.00am the first sound was always of birds singing. Like clockwork one particular bird could be heard every single morning without fail, at exactly the same time.

After sunrise you could see thousands of small birds flying in different groups, a bevy here, a bevy there, in all directions, in the countryside where we lived. One day you notice nest building. Another day you notice a kite perched on the highest point of the tallest tree ready to pounce on our chicks. We kept hens, laying about a dozen eggs and chicks hatching after 21 days. The hen with her chicks would then walk around in the garden to feed on insects. This was when the chicks were exposed to danger. Many times a hen would lose as many as ten out of twelve chicks to these kites. It was only when the chicks are six to eight weeks old that they would be safe. The kite would only take very small birds.

The biggest danger, however, was the wild cats. A wild cat could even attack the adult chicken.

My best memory is the weaver birds colony. Just behind our house in a big tree, suddenly, weaver birds started building nests. I watched the entire operation as it happened lasting about a week. The comings and goings of these beautiful black and yellow birds carrying straws in their beaks, the noise as they flew in 20s and 30s at a time, the delicate job they carried on weaving nests, was worth watching hours on end. This I did all the time.

There were other bigger birds one could kill for food. My favourite was the guinea fowl. Second favourite was the dove. Boys quite often hunted these with catapults. It was not easy. I tried this lots of times with no success. But in our village a boy called simply Yokaana was exceptional. I saw him at least once a week carrying a number of doves he had just killed with the aid of a catapult. Could be three, five or more. One time he passed near our house with ten birds.

In spite of having no luck hunting birds, I did not give up entirely. One evening I heard sounds of guinea fowls down in our banana plantation. Armed with a catapult I rushed to the area. I noticed 20 or 30 of these birds about 30 to 50 yards away making big noises as they always did. They were messing around on the ground. I loaded my catapult with a good stone aimed and released the stone. Instantly the birds flew away as they always did. But one did not. I had got a direct hit on its head. I ran to it and caught it with a little struggle and took it home. When mother and the rest of the family saw me bringing home the bird they could not believe their eyes. The all knew how hopeless I was to try hunting guinea fowls with a catapult. Nobody ever gave me a chance of success. Even Yokaana. He never killed one. The only birds he killed were doves. Nobody else ever killed a guinea fowl in our village with a catapult as far as I can remember.

In normal circumstances to kill guinea fowls, you required a rifle and a game licence. My grand father had one, like most of the chiefs. Almost every week-end he went hunting bringing home a few birds at a time. His main pastime, however, was the big game. With a gang of men, grandfather could disappear for days in the jungle only to return with a carcass of a buffalo, smoke dried by his gang. He often distributed meat to friends and relatives for which he became very popular.

One incident I did not witness, but remember a vivid story told by one of my cousins. The story goes that one night, two buffaloes fought in our garden and one was killed in the fight.

So there was suddenly plenty of meat. Our parents gave some of it away to friends and relatives. Grandfather is said to have asked my father where he got that special power, kind of voodoo, to have a buffalo killed without a gun or spear, when it took him days travelling to where the animals roamed. My father did neither of those. A kill for him was done while he slept. Something unheard of! And our area was not known to have buffaloes around. How these two or maybe three came to be there remained a mystery.

Growing up, we never saw wild animals. To see them you had to go to the National Parks, a long way from where I lived. The nearest encounter was the sound from a laughing hyena one evening. I vaguely remember this. About the same time hyenas killed and ate two lambs belonging to a relative. They dug a hole at the back of the kitchen, where the sheep and lambs are kept   at night, and took away the two lambs.

The other thing of interest I remember very early on in life was nothing to do with animals. This involved bad people visiting our house when our parents were not at home. I might have been two or three. Our parents normally went to work on the farm first thing in the morning, leaving us kids at home alone. I don't remember which of my brother or sister was with me. Mother had left food cooking so that on return we could have dinner. But before our parents returned, two men walked into the house, put food on the table and ate it. Then they went into our parents' bedroom and walked out with a suitcase full of mum's clothing. On their way out they left a message for our parents with us kids. The message was that they had taken what belonged to them. When we told the story to our parents it was a shock to them. Our parents told us that the men were not friends. They were bad people. They were thieves. These thieves had stolen mum's clothes. As children, we regarded anyone coming in the house as a friend and a good person. That was our first experience of bad people. On that day at least I added one word to my vocabulary and that word was "thief". It was the first time I heard of the word. This happened at Buseesa where we had our first home. It was about 100 metres from school.

Later father gave the land to the church and a church was built in the same place as our home had been. We moved to Ibulanku two miles away, where we had a larger acreage of land. This was now our new home.

We must have been unfortunate in attracting thieves. They say history never repeats itself, well it did. The thieves visited us once again at our new home of Ibulanku. They stole my new school uniform. This was the best uniform I remember having. Weeks before mother and I had walked to Iganga, 11 miles away, to buy the Khaki material from which a local tailor made the uniform for me - made to measure. The thieves also took mother's clothing in a suitcase. They also took the best china and cutlery from a cupboard. Both china (three dozen pieces) and cutlery were used only for visitors and were always locked away.

That particular night mother was away attending her father's funeral at Bumpingo. In those days after burials people stayed at the house for weeks. Mother always came home in the morning. It was only two miles away. One Sunday morning she came home and six of us kids, some from the neighbourhood, were still asleep. and the sun had already risen.

Mother realised that thieves had visited us once again, although there was no sign of a break-in. Maybe we did not bolt the door. Mother checked everything and was able to account for all that had been stolen,

To make matters worse, somebody came in - a man - claiming he could, with the power of magic, catch the thieves. First he wanted to determine in which direction the thieves went after stealing. He asked mother for a bowl three-quarters full of water. He then placed three matchsticks in the water in the bowl. To our amazement the matchsticks moved from one side of the bowl to the other. At this stage the man with his pointing finger, said the direction of the sticks showed that the thieves went that way, adding that he would be able to catch them. But time was crucial, he had to go immediately. He finally said there were at least three thieves. So he was going to find three of his mates to apprehend these thieves and it would take about three days, at least. Mother paid him some money. I don't know how much. We never saw him again - never trust a stranger. But in a desperate situation one is sometimes forced to do anything.

Grandfather died about five years after father. During that time we partly depended on grandfather for school fees. It was the time when we were all small kids with very little input in the farm work. So his death was a severe blow to us all.

Yokaana Wakibi Kakaire Kitikyamwogo (grandfather) was simply known as Yokaana Wakibi. He was a very kind man but I don't remember seeing him smile. But I do remember him saying that grandchildren were the best thing in his life. Nothing pleased him as much as seeing his grandchildren playing around him. And he had quite a lot. I happen to be the **seventh** grandchild and born in the seventh month. Yokaana Wakibi had several wives, and apart from one, all had children. I remember at least eight names of his wives. The estimated number of children was 36. He was not what you would call a polygamist extraordinaire. He was a normal polygamist as, at the time, amongst men, chiefs in particular, it was fashionable to have several wives.

I remember his black car. Driven by one of his sons, Saul. Yokaana Wakibi regularly came to our house to check on us. The car was one of those making the sound of a motor bike. It must have been an air cooled engine. It had what you call a two stroke engine. Because of the sound the car made, it was nicknamed tututu (tototo). The **first** time grandmother had a ride she was sick. There was an unpleasant smell from the engine. But what I remember most is grandma's story describing her **first** experience of a car ride. In her words, "As the car started moving, trees, houses, bushes, everything - even cows - were running past us in opposite direction." She had never seen a car in her life before and the **first** time she saw one, she had a ride in it.. You can imagine the situation, the conversation between grandpa and grandma just before getting into the car and sitting down for her first ride. She was already an old woman in her late 50/60's, which in those days was quite something.

There was yet another *first experience* story not to be missed. This involved a young man travelling to South Africa from the Congo to attend a Boy Scout Jamboree via Uganda. It was a record breaking of so many "**firsts**". First it was the first time he left the country. He travelled by road covering

1,000 miles to Kampala on the back of lorries (several of them). The young man's second **'first'** was the sight of a train in Kampala. Standing at platform 1 at Kampala Railway Station the young man was spellbound, mesmerised, to see the 17 coach train - just the size of it was to him out of this world. His third **'first'** was then to travel on it, to Nairobi. This was a 24 hour journey. His fourth 'first' was seeing an aeroplane at Embakasi Airport, Nairobi now Jomo Kenyatta Airport. The **'fifth'** was flying in an aeroplane. It was one of the most unusual experiences, having five 'firsts' in a matter of days. This takes an average person years.

Grandpa was always travelling but never alone. Apart from his son, the driver, there was a man by the name of Katumba. In those days, being related or just a friend to someone did not make much sense or difference, so whether Katumba was grandpa's friend or a relative didn't matter. Everywhere grandpa travelled Katumba was in tow. Katumba did all the talking and made everyone laugh. You could say Katumba was grandfather's personal full time comedian. Katumba made so many laugh that every one listening to him wanted to stay in his company as long as it was possible. Come to think of it I was not aware of him having a family. I don't think he had one.

He wasn't in employment. He was in unpaid entertainment, and seemed to enjoy every minute of it. It was not unusual for someone in those days to provide a free service to a chief in return for free meals, free accommodation, and sometimes old clothing. Just being in the company of someone famous was in itself satisfying. After all there were no jobs around. Almost everybody worked for oneself on their own farm, producing their own food. People grew their own food, kept chickens, goats and sheep, and needed little else. One would sell vegetables ,eggs fruit etc by standing on the road at a certain place, to motorists mainly Asians - they controlled the economy and all shops in towns belonged to them. The basics like sugar, salt and soap were not expensive. You could sell one basket of fruit, or a dozen eggs, and be able to buy a month's supply of basics easily. Its true there was poverty but not the kind of poverty where people went hungry. And most important people were always happy. Some were even getting drunk every day. No employment, no regular, reliable income. Yet life went on very well for these people. No worries. People helped each other in case of trouble. And if you saw anyone breaking into your house (usually at night) all you did was to shout a loud alarm, and within minutes neighbours would arrive to catch the burglar. Caught red handed, the burglar would be subjected to social justice on the spot. Sometimes the burglar would be very badly beaten, even to death. What you would call jungle law. Not as wide spread as it sounds, rather exceptional. There were no police of any kind. The Chiefs did not object and the public were in full support. At the same time there was full co-operation among neighbours. If you needed anything all you had to do was ask and, would be given. So there was no excuse to break into someone's house to steal.

Unfortunately, things changed slowly but dramatically. There was a change of thinking on materialism. More and more individual wealth set in, so much that there was increased robbery and less and less help from neighbours. This started worrying everyone and trust did suffer. You then could no longer trust a neighbour. At one point, robbery started. At its worst, what started as simple robbery developed into armed robbery. Living in a small society everybody knew everybody and as robbers didn't wear any balaclava in those days, they could be identified, followed, and their house noted.

In one area in Busoga District robbery had reached such an alarming scale that one particular chief swore to do whatever it takes to eliminate it. Having failed in his effort, the chief resulted to drastic measures. But he went too far. He ordered what was called "Mizindula". This involved carrying out an act of killing the armed robbers. The chief made an order to surprise any suspected armed robber while still at his home and kill him before he could go out and commit the crime of which he was suspected.

The county was under British rule, then. On direct orders from the Governor, the chief was arrested. He was tried and found guilty and sentenced to a maximum security jail for five years. The public, however, supported his act 100%. The situation had gone far beyond control. Those who's relatives and friends had been murdered by these armed robbers said William Wilberforce Nadiope had done the right thing and was always in their mind. To these people it should be a tooth for a tooth. On his release from jail there were celebrations all over the county. He became very popular, and when it came to elections of Kyabazinga (the top chief in the whole District of Busoga) he was elected unopposed. In his campaign he said the county needed a strong ruler to fight crime in all its guises. Ordinary people had complete trust in him.

Nadiope became a very popular and good administrator and even the British government recognised his brilliant work. He was knighted. He came to be known as Sir William

Wilberforce Nadiope.

Sir William was of stocky build with receding hair and was full of energy. He was a first class communicator, like Winston Churchill, but without his education, or his wealth. This was a very practical man who spent most of his spare time messing about with his cars. He had several. If you went to his house on a Saturday afternoon you would find a man dressed in blue overalls working on his cars, always making sure they were all checked and serviced and cleaned regularly. He would be changing spark plugs, changing tyres, changing oil or just washing the car. He was unique. He was the only man known to service his own car though he was a top chief who could afford to pay someone else to do the job. The rest of the chiefs always sent their cars with drivers to garages and wait for the bill.

I was able to visit his house once when I was working as a tractor salesman. Sir William was also a farmer in his own right. Whilst there I had one or two big surprises. The two of us were seated in his gigantic lounge which was fully furnished. He sat on the opposite side with a small table between us. On the table was a tea pot and one cup of tea and a milk jug. He kept talking to me as he drank his tea. He did not offer me anything although I had come from about 80 miles away. This is only time ever I remember visiting someone and not being offered at least a drink. The second surprise, he took me outside just to show me his proud work. He had just finished digging his own grave. He said at least he knew where he would at last "retire" and from his own sweat. Nobody in the whole world I know or heard of, had ever done this. That was Sir William Wilberforce Nadiope. I wonder what was written on the head stone of his grave.

This may seem a long story and a lot of information I gave to old Albert. It is, however, not the end. Albert, after a few weeks, came back with another idea.

He wanted to explore more about the *numbers* related to me and my family. He could be researching something for himself or for someone else, I thought. I really did not know nor did I have the courage to ask him why. I trusted him. It was a question of trust. The man was on his last legs - not long to live. Had he been a young man I probably would not trust him and would not give him as much information as I did. At that stage I would do anything for Albert. I could not think of any particular number, but he reminded me of the **seven** I talked about earlier, being the seventh grandchild on my mother's side and born in the seventh month. What followed amazed me. Facts relating to number seven in my life began to emerge.

First, my real girl friend happened to come from a family of seven - two males and five females. There were four daughters and a son, the last born. The address was No 17. We got married in 1967 on December 16th (1 + 6 = 7). She was 25 and me 34
(2 + 5= 7); (3 + 4 = 7).

We lived in Uganda from 1968 to 1979 when we came back to the UK.

Our house number is 197, which could also be interpreted as 17, ie 1 + 9 + 7 = 17. For her it was home from home.

Our first born - a boy, was born in 1968, 6 + 8 = 14, ie 2 x 7. The second born - a girl - was born in 1970, 10 x7. My wife was born in 1942, 42 = 6 x 7. Mother and son share 42 and 68. When the mother was 68 the son was 42.

Year wife was born 1942--1+9+4+2=16, 1+6=7
Year I was born   1933---1+9+3+3=16, 1+6=7

This year 2013 as I write this book, our combined age (family) 43+45+71+80=239=2+3+9=14=2x7

The other day I was looking for some information in the solar system to see if something relevant to our common 7 could be found. There was not much but I should comment on the little found. The most that caught my eye was in relation to the planets orbiting the sun. This is what I found out and was really impressed.

I picked out three planets: our Earth, Mars, and the tiny Pluto which is farthest from the sun.

Orbiting the Sun,
The Earth takes 365 days = 3+6+5=14=2x7.
        Mars takes 687 days = 6+8+7=21=3x7.
Pluto takes 248 years. Yes you read it correctly, 248 years and 197   days
248 years--2+4+8=14=2x7.

The 197 has already been taken care of.
The figure 7 is still there.

Perhaps something here needs an explanation. For example how come Pluto takes so long to orbit the sun while Earth and Mars both take a much shorter time.

The reason is simple. The distance from the sun varies widely. Earth is only 93,000,000 miles away from the sun. Mars is further away 154,730,000 miles. The tiny Pluto orbits the sun by a much longer distance away. And that is a whopping 4,538,910,000 miles from the sun. That's the reason for the 248 years and 197 days it takes Pluto to orbit the sun.

Here again I tried to work out on these distances to see if there was any relevance to our now famous 7. By adding these distances I got the following results.

Distances in miles from the sun:
Earth   93,000,000
Mars   154,730,000
Pluto   4,538,910,000

Total distance 4,786,640,000

Adding: 4+7+8+6+6+4+6+6+4=35 = 5x7

One other point of interest is that our house number and the total surface area of the earth both have a common figure - 197. However, the earth's 197,000,000 surface area square miles is a million times our house number - 197.

Seven still rules! Having looked at these figures several

times, I did not think much about them. I concluded that they were just figures with no real meaning. These figures are just coincidences, simple mathematics, and not a mathematical marvel or magic; and certainly no fortune can be made from them. Just in case some people were thinking of linking these figures with anything like that. But then you never know people. We are all different. I said to old Albert that there must be thousands of people in a similar category. I did not think I was unique.

Albert seemed to think otherwise, and suggested that he takes time to think of what these numbers could mean. I waited for interpretation but instead Albert had yet another question. He wanted to know in which order the girls in my wife's family were married. It happened to be that the first to get married was the youngest. The second born still remained second. The first born came third while the third born came fourth. I asked Albert if that made any sense to him. To me, like the numbers earlier they made no sense - pure coincidence I still maintained.

Albert still thought there must be something in these. Then he wanted to know dates of birth, only the months of all the girls from my wife's family and my family. I started wondering whether Albert was really digging up something strange - some kind of surprise. It was difficult to comprehend. I had read from newspapers about stars. I was never a believer in stars as portrayed in the daily papers. I still don't. My thinking was that Albert was going to interpret dates of birth into something similar to what the daily papers write - about star signs. There was no way I could be persuaded to change my mind. I did trust Albert but on this occasion there was no way I could believe anything of that kind from him. But that was not the case. No reference to stars came forward.

One evening while in the Inn, Albert leaned over and said a word in my ear. He said he had a secret for me. I said I was listening. He went on to say I must trust him to the end, and a secret is a secret and will always be. "SO BE IT" was my comment.

Twenty five years after we left Uganda, we made our first visit to the country. And that was in 2005. There were four of us then in 1979 when we came to the UK. In 2005 we had become **seven**. Our daughter, her husband, and their two children, our son, and us two that makes **seven**. If you are thinking we might have planned our visit to coincide with the years 2005 and 25, and family extension to seven I can assure you that nothing like that was the case. Trust me.

We went to Uganda in 2005 to attend a wedding of my nephew Timothy. You will have noticed that Timothy happens to have seven letters in his name.

It was a three weeks holiday, but me and our son Mark stayed a further ten days due to some mix-up in our visa. One afternoon in a coffee bar next to Egypt Airlines, I met a most interesting man. Introducing himself as Jimmy he said he thought he recognised me. Adding that he came from Masaka and went to Masaka Primary and Kitovu College. At this point it came clear to me that it was unlikely we ever met. My Primary School Buseesa is 188 miles away. So I asked him if he ever was a cub or a boy scout, which he was. I noticed that

Jimmy was really loud as we talked. While camping as a cub I noticed one boy who was really loud and I wondered whether it could be him. And it was him, but he looked so different from what I remembered.

Listening to Jimmy's details of camping experiences at Kazi the camping site near Entebbe, I remembered almost all that we had been through those many years ago. It must be at least 65 years ago. We had a moving conversation about the memories of our experiences as young boys.

We both remembered a song **Kiarama: Kiarama Kiarama Kiarama Shokere** in the camp. We sung many songs but this became so popular and that's why we still remembered the words after such a long time. It was the song to open the camp in the morning, and the song to close the camp before bed time. Unfortunately none of us knew what these words meant. We did not ask.

As a resident of Kampala, I expected Jimmy to have a wide knowledge of the city. Having been away so long I asked him if he could tell me everything about the city. Starting rather slowly and quieter than usual he wanted to know if I wanted a long or a short answer. I wanted all and everything. I wanted to know what Kampala means to him: was my reply.

Jimmy proceeded to give me the detailed long answer I required. Here it is.

Kampala is a very beautiful city as you know. But it is its suburbs that make it what it is. Amin tried to destroy Kampala and its people especially Baganda. We have made a lot of progress since he was overthrown. We had a terrible time. We experienced the worst that I can remember in living memory. Never had we experienced such commodity shortage in this country.

Kampala means Kololo, Katwe, Kabaalagal-Kansanga.

Kampala means Kasubi, Kamwokya, Kawanda, Kawempe.

Kampala means, Kibuli, Kibuye, Kireka, Kyambogo

Kampala means Mengo, Makerere, Makindie, Mutundwe.

Kampala means Mbuya, Mulago, Muyenga, Munyonyo.

Kampala means Portbell, Home of Uganda Waragi - Uganda's best and most popular drink.

Kampala means Luzira, where the worst of the baddies are banded together and locked away.

Kampala means, Lugogo Sports complex popular for pastime watching or playing your favourite sport.

Kampala means Lubaga Catholic Cathedral for spiritual guidance and worship.

So that is Kampala K-M-P-L for you Mr Ignatius.

He went on: And there is more. There is the "N" factor. Hundreds of women have N initial. Names like Nambi, Nakiyaga, Nanjobe, Namakula, Nalumansi, Nansamba,

Namuli, Namayanja, Namusoke, Nagawa, are common.

In the same way you have many places starting with N like: Najanankumbi, Natete, Namirembe, Nakulabye, Nakivubo, Nakasero, Nakawa, Ntinda, Naguru, Namboole, Namuwongo
.

I bet you have nothing even close to this kind of situation where you come from. I challenge you to produce names just like these we have in and around Kampala.

After a pause I told Jimmy that I was ready for a duel. *And this was my response.* The place where I was brought up is called Ibulanku. My first name is Ignatius. North of Ibulanku is Ibako where my Uncle Ham lived. Continuing east of Ibako you come to Idudi a fast growing shopping centre. If you do a U-turn you come to Iganga where I attended secondary school education. Farther ahead of Iganga is Igenge. Uncles Walukamba and Wakabi had homes there.

Starting from Ibulanku again, this time going south, Igombe-Bukabega is not far. This is where Yokonia Kibedi Zirabamuzale, one of my great uncles, lived. He was a well known and respected administrator as Secretary General of Busoga. Yokonia is reputed for being the first man in Busoga to grasp the English Language at the highest level and was responsible for all translations and interpretations of English/Luganda at the time when not many Ugandans could understand the English language. Uganda is a former British Colony and as such the rulers needed to communicate with the ruled. The rulers could not speak Luganda, so they had to find local people who spoke English for translation.

Farther west you come to Isikiro, Ibanga, and Ivugunhu. I
have a special interest in these last three places as I will explain
in a moment. The three places have in common Is and Ts. I
call them the three "IT"

Isikiro is home of a friend late Tewungwa.

Ibanga was home of   uncle late Taibu

Ivugunhu is where I had a very good friend Tabingwa.

Re-writing in brief we have:

Isikiro -Tewungwa

Ivugunhu - Tabingwa

Ibanga -Taibu

Another example is Buseesa my place of birth. Some
places of interest near by include Buwoya, Buyanga, Buigula,
Bumpingo, Butende, Busoola, Busolera all starting with B like
Buseesa.

Just one other little thing, Iganga where I attended
secondary school the teachers were "Mus" Musumba,
Mulwanyi, Mukumbya, and Mudumba. At the same time in
town, there this was a most popular Asian named Mafudu. He
was chubby, bare footed with a beer belly and bald head.
Mafudu was the only man with his own water well in his yard.
His shop being at the end of town there was plenty of space for
his business. He was a hot chilli merchant. In his yard you
would see red chilli spread out on concrete ground to dry in the
sun. Occasionally he would be seen picking unwanted foreign
objects from the drying pepper. No one wanted to be near his
drying pepper as it could make you sneeze uncomfortably, and

so rarely did Mafudu have visitors. But the locals from whom he bought pepper for his business, liked him as, unlike other Asian shop keepers, he spoke the local language fluently and so was regarded as one of them. This was the time when shop keepers in Uganda were almost 100% Asians. The other M was Mr. Makanga the only black man owning a lorry truck.

As you can see Jimmy all these are pure coincidences, and could be found anywhere for no particular reason. No magic and certainly no fortune can be made out of them.

So Jimmy I am afraid your story about Kampala, its suburbs, ladies' names and all that you have told me, don't mean much to me. It could be found anywhere in the world. All you have to do is to look round and you will be amazed with what can be found.

While Jimmy was still thinking about what I had just said, and maybe comment, some one came in and joined our table. He was Jimmy's dad. Jimmy introduced me as a friend from England. Dr. Festo Katongole-Musoke was a retired for twenty years. Noticing his lack of interest in what we were talking about, I changed the subject. I asked him about Uganda under Museveni. I wanted to know the overall picture - the minuses and plusses or whatever as some people have said. Suddenly he came very much alive saying it was a very good question and proceeded to give a long answer.

His words
Amini expelled Uganda Asians. Museveni brought in non Ugandan Asians and more, much more. By attracting multinational business communities from all over the world:

78

Asia, America, China, South Africa, Saud Arabia the United Kingdom and every where, the country is once again now on its feet walking. Before we were down not on our feet but on our back unable to stand. Uganda is now like where you now live in England. Hundreds of companies have invested heavily in this country and all this is due to trust of the Government. There can never be investment without trust. Believe me my friend. Visiting England about ten years ago I noticed so many multinational businesses every where. The commonest example I saw was KFC and McDonalds. These could be found even in the smallest place. I know these are American Franchises, found all over the world. But they form part of business community useful for development.

The doctor continued with quite a different story. A story that, I thought was, about President Museveni. He went on: *You may be surprised about this. Pay particular attention to what I am about to say. Did you, or did it ever occur to you that Museveni, I mean the name Museveni was or could be of Italian origin? I met one Italian years back. He spoke of the naming of Mountains of the Moon. The very first men to reach the summit of Rwenzori were Italians. They actually gave it the name Mountains of the Moon. One of the Italian men is said to have been a distant relative of Mussolini. The name Mussolini became very popular. But when it came to writing it down the reporter dropped the second "s." He wrote "Musolini.* Then, strangely, Musolini became Museveni

MUSEVENI
MUSOLINI

The one Italian Mussolini I remember, was also known as

Benito, the founder of a fascist movement, Prime Minister and dictator in Italy for I think 23 years. Anyway all the same I thought it was an amusing story. Whether it was true or not I can't be sure. The possibility of being just pure coincidence cannot be ruled out. Next time I am in the vicinity of the Mountains of the Moon I will look for the elderly with a chance of throwing more light on the subject.

I think this is just a STORY. I might be able to tell you more about this, next time around.

From time man has been on earth, superstition has ruled the world. Religion and superstition were one and the same, both being based on unscientific unproved theories from our ancestors. But during 16 and 17 centuries, scientists were exploring the natural world with ever increasing curiosity. As a result the inevitable clash occurred between religion and science. The top religious leaders had very strong views about the world. At one time they believed that the world was flat and that if you went far enough you would fall off the edge. When the question of relation between the earth and the sun was raised they believed that the sun revolved round the earth. Then came a scientist - mathematician/astronomer by the name Galileo Galilei. He told the world that the earth orbits the sun contrary to the view held by religious leaders. They believed in the opposite and were so infuriated that Galileo Galilei was persecuted. His crime was contradiction to the teaching not only in Rome but also the Bible scriptures, that the Sun revolves round the Earth. We must remember that at the time Religion was Government and very powerful. Only a handful of people had scientific knowledge, so masses followed the powerful religious leaders without question. So the idea of a round world revolving round the sun did not appeal to the people. In practice, to be honest, it is not difficult to convince the uneducated that the earth is not only flat but that it is in fact stationary and the sun just raises from the east in the morning and sets down disappearing in the west - a daily routine. This theory would be more convincing in the tropics on the equator where not only do you have equal hours day and night but also the sun follows the same path east to west all year round.

Superstition with numbers has been with us for quite a long time. In the west, number 13, even now still regarded as unlucky. No one wants a house number 13. But people now are moving away from this belief. And I am sure the British now in the year 2013, regard the number 13 as lucky particularly with regard to sport. After 77 years trying to win the Wimbledon Tennis Championship it is in this year 2013 that they finally got Andy Murray as a winner. And in Rugby, the Lions did it too this year in Australia also after a very long time. And the arrival of Prince George of Cambridge, third in line to be King of United Kingdom could not be at a better time.

But still there is a large number of people worrying about number 13. Real fear of 13 exists. And the word used to describe this fear is a 17 letter word known as - *triskaidekaphobia.*

The ancient Chinese regarded odd numbers as female and therefore luckier and even numbers male and unlucky. Number one was as the indivisible number of divine unity, while two is a link between God and man and a pair of humans and three (the number of Holy Trinity) has always been regarded lucky. A four shaped pattern, (four leaf clover like preferred) means perfection. But don't tell the Chinese. To the Chinese it has a sound of death.

Both the ancient Egyptians and Babylonians believed number 7 (the total sum of 3 and 4), to be lucky because it was the number of sacred planets.

In the Genesis book of the Bible, we are told that Noah, apart from his three sons, Shem, Ham, and Japheth, their wives and their children, led **seven** pairs of clean animals, one pair of every unclean animal and **seven** pairs of clean birds into the ark. After the floods had gone down, God, who had created the world in **seven** days, sent a redeeming rainbow with **seven** colours.

A person with strong belief in religion and superstition in equal measure, (and plenty of such people exist), will come to a conclusion linking the Almighty God in heaven with the number **seven**. And that is the strength and power of **seven** linked to superstition. Lots of people have complete *Trust in it.*

Superstition has been with us in the past, is here today and will be in the future, *always, to control the unscientific and non-analytical mind.*

Acknowledgement

Tribute goes to my daughter Sara, and to wife Patricia for taking trouble of   proof reading and typing the manuscript.
I also wish to thank all my family and friends for encouragement. It took me a long time before finally sitting down to the job in my eightieth year.